The Berisheet
END-TIMES PASSOVER PROPHECY

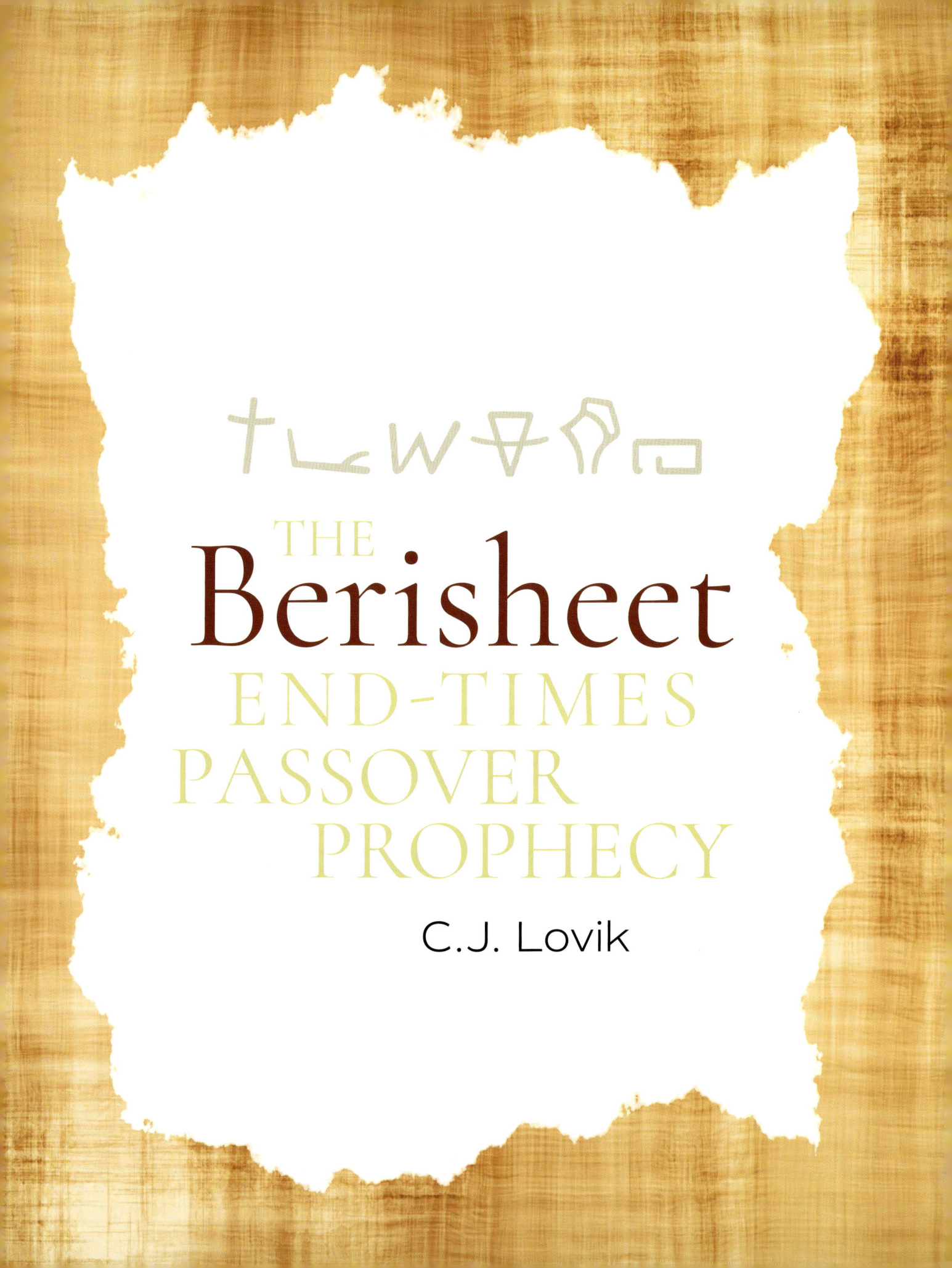

C.J. Lovik

www.lighthouse.pub

Visit our website
to purchase books and preview
upcoming titles.

Contact us at:
feedback@lighthouse.pub

Copyright © 2020, C.J. Lovik
All rights reserved.
Second Edition.

Cover Design and Interior Layout by Sergio E. León

Sergio was born and raised in Mexico City, where he studied Design and Arts in the National Autonomous University of Mexico (UNAM). For nearly 21 years, Sergio has worked in a variety of positions, primarily acting as Art and Design Director for major brands and publications. Today, Sergio is the Art and Design Director for Lighthouse Gospel Beacon, where he is responsible for all digital and print media. Every day, Sergio is growing in Christ while continuing to produce art and media to help illustrate the love of the Savior. Sergio is married to his wonderful wife, Monica, and they have two amazing children.

Table of Contents

Foreword 6

Chapter 1
The First Prophecy "In the Beginning" 8

Chapter 2
The Rapture and the Second Coming 26

Chapter 3
The Berisheet End-Times Passover Prophecy 54

Chapter 4
Sabbath-Millennial Prophetic Perspective 78

Chapter 5
The First Two Beginnings 102

Chapter 6
4004 BC - The Date of Creation?........................**108**

Chapter 7
How Long was Adam in the Garden?.................**118**

Chapter 8
33 Years - The Unwitting Witness.......................**136**

Chapter 9
30 AD - The Last Adam Succeeds!.....................**144**

Chapter 10
Pattern is Prophecy..**160**

Chapter 11
The End!..**168**

Chapter 12
Where will you spend Eternity?..........................**184**

FOREWORD

How many time spans has the Lord decreed in order to accomplish his purposes and plans? How many prophecies are hidden in plain sight in the days, week, months and years that the Lord prescribed for his creation?

Explore the "once a week" prophetic harbinger that has been repeated over 300,000 times, just waiting to be ultimately fulfilled. The seventh day—the day of completion and rest—has been recognized as a shadow/type for millennia.

Where can we find the prophecy that is casting this long shadow over man's historical time-line? Does it predict that after six days—6000 years—the time allowed for man to work comes to an end and the 1000 years set aside for the rule of Christ on the earth begins?

Are we just a few more tic-tocks away from a brand-new dispensation of time, one prophesied hundreds of times in the Old Testament that has sadly been allegorized into something it was never meant to be by the anti-supernaturalists and metaphorists?

Is Christ's kingdom about to impose itself supernaturally on this world just as the Lord predicted it would?

Is there a prophecy found in the first word in the bible that discloses the most important event to ever take place on the earth?

Discover the message God has hidden in plain sight in Genesis 1:1. Is this the Proto-Evangelium that precedes the Messianic prophecy found in Genesis 3:15?

Does this Genesis 1:1 Divine disclosure also establish the timing of all the Messianic epochs from creation to the eternal state? Have parts of this prophetic time-line already been fulfilled? Are you living in the terminal generation? What Terminates? What begins?

We cannot know the "day or the hour," but can we know the season that alerts us to look up with eyes of faith as our redeemer is about to gloriously appear in the clouds.

Are you inhabited by the Blessed Hope?

Are you prepared for the events that are on the razor's edge of fulfillment?

CHAPTER 1

The First Prophecy
"In the Beginning"

Samaritan Inscription containing a portion of the Bible in nine lines of Hebrew text, currently housed in the British Museum.

Did God reveal to the prophet Isaiah a clue as to where we might find the very first and most amazing prophecy ever revealed in the Bible?

Listen to Isaiah 46:9-10 and see if you can discover the clue that unlocks the mystery location of the Berisheet Prophecy.

> *Remember the former things of old:*
> *for I am God, and there is none else;*
> *I am God, and there is none like me,*
> **Declaring the end from the beginning,**
> *and from ancient times the things that are not yet done, saying,*
> *My counsel shall stand, and I will do all my pleasure:*

Were there events ordained in Heaven, events that, both have and will, unfold on the earth?

Were there events that were declared by God in the beginning—events that will at the appointed time end one epoch in man's history as they begin another?

If God's words are to be taken literally, then where might we find this amazing revelation?

Our search begins with the very first word that God revealed in the Scripture.

This revelation was disclosed in the language we know as Hebrew. The only language in the world that is actually three languages in one.

Hebrew is composed of 22 pictograms that are symbols or letters meant to be assembled to form IDEAS that we call WORDS.

Hebrew is also a NUMBER language. Each of the 22 pictograms is also a number denominated by God, each number having a meaning based on how that number is used in the Bible.

Finally, we have the Phonetic Hebrew language, the oldest language in the world, a language that has been miraculously preserved and is spoken today by a people who have been miraculously preserved and are living once again, after thousands of years of dispersion, in the only place on the earth that God gave as an inheritance to His particular people.

The existence of Israel and the preservation of the Hebrew language is proof positive that you can take the Word of God literally. It is not a testimony as some erroneously presume to the resilience and faith of an oppressed nation, it is a testimony to the faithfulness and dependability of God.

Take a look at a graphic representation of the very first word that God spoke to Moses the prophet who chiseled it into stone, letter by letter over 3400 years ago.

Keep in mind that Hebrew is written from right to left.

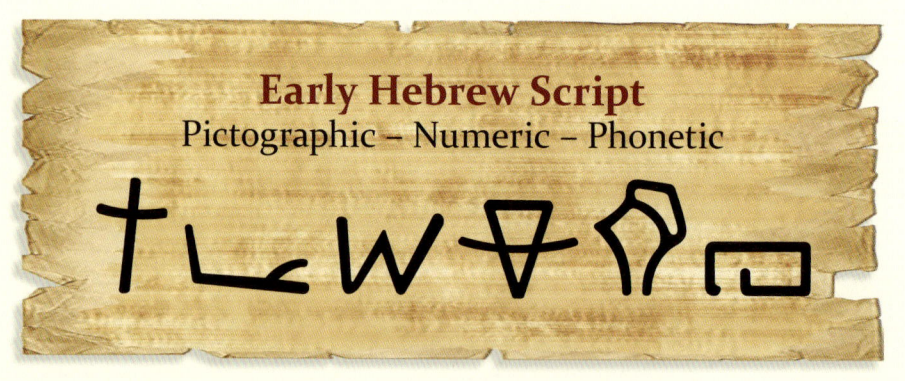

Early Hebrew Script
Pictographic – Numeric – Phonetic

Do you recognize the very first word revealed in the Bible?

Perhaps you do not recognize the Hebrew Script as it was scribed before the Babylonian Captivity.

I have chosen to disclose this letter by letter, picture by picture and number by number revelation in the most probable way that it would have appeared to Moses. Moses would not be able to read Modern Post Babylonian Exile Hebrew, I am certain he could easily read the script as presented in this book.

Based on several years of research, this is probably as close to the script or pictograms that were common when Moses wrote the Torah, dictated by God letter by letter.

You are, of course, looking at Berisheet, the Hebrew Word we translate into English as IN THE BEGINNING found in Genesis 1:1.

It is in this single word BERISHEET that is translated literally as IN BEGINNING that we will discover what God revealed about the END from the beginning.

In order to recognize the prophetic significance of the six letter Hebrew word Berisheet, we need to figure out the meaning of each of the six letters or Pictograms that were from the very beginning, and are to this day, embedded in the language that God created in order to reveal His Living WORD to mankind.

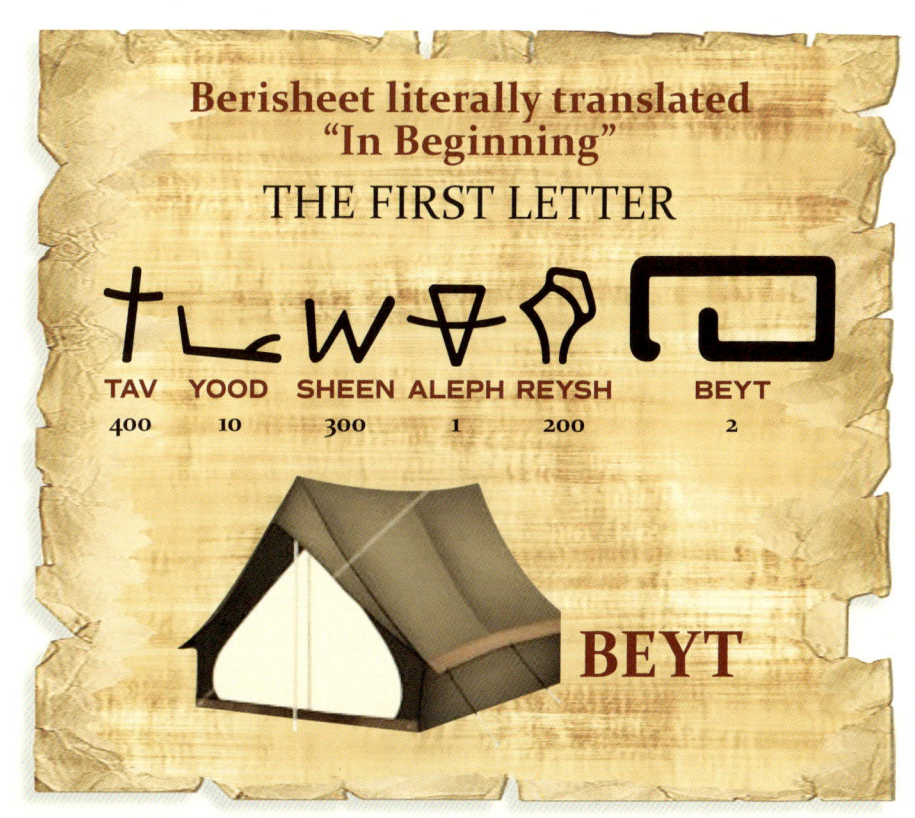

Berisheet literally translated "In Beginning"

THE FIRST LETTER

TAV	YOOD	SHEEN	ALEPH	REYSH	BEYT
400	10	300	1	200	2

BEYT

Beyt is the very first letter or pictogram revealed in God's Word.

Beyt is the pictogram of the floor plan of a house or tent.

Beyt was disclosed to put into man's mind the first idea that God headlined as one of the central themes of His revelation. The idea of HOME.

Think about it!

The very first pictographic letter that God reveals to man introduces the concept of HOME.

Beyt is also the number 2.

Let's begin unfolding the first and perhaps the most amazing revelation ever disclosed in the Bible by asking the one question every child would ask if he saw a picture of a Tent.

Who is Inside the Tent?

Who is Inside the Tent?

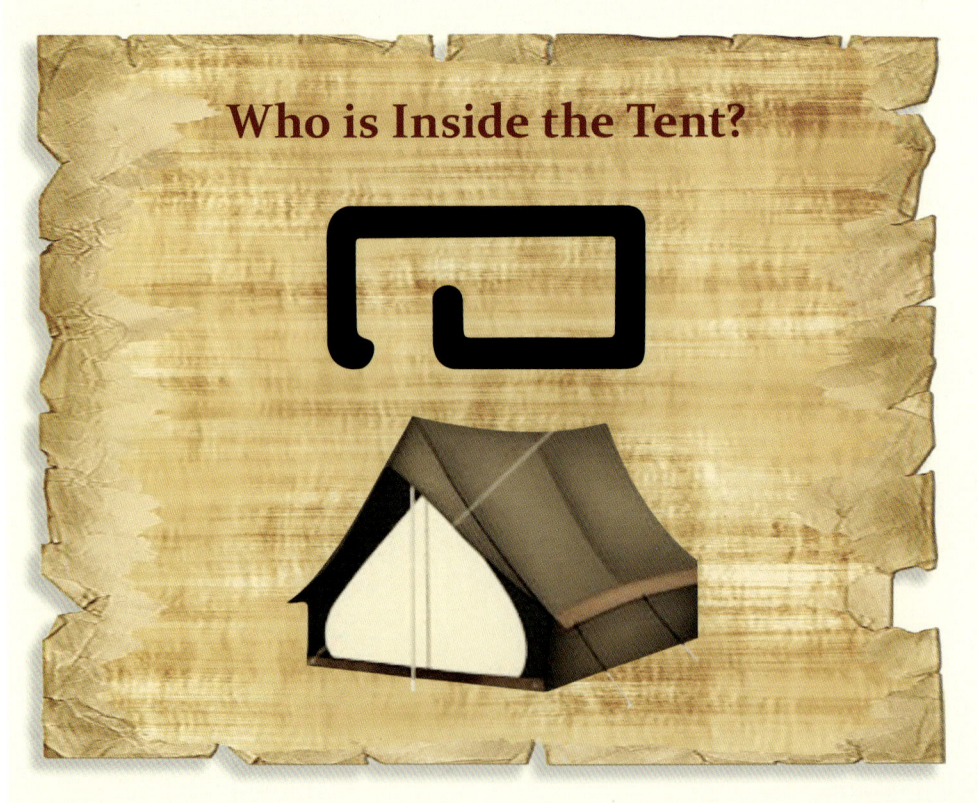

The letter Beyt, pictured as a Tent, is also the one letter in Hebrew that is literally translated as IN or INSIDE.

So perhaps asking who is IN or INSIDE the Tent is not such a silly question.

Just Who **IS** inside the Tent?

Perhaps the next Hebrew letter will give us a clue!

Berisheet literally translated "In Beginning"

THE SECOND LETTER

TAV	YOOD	SHEEN	ALEPH	REYSH	BEYT
400	10	300	1	200	2

REYSH

The letter Reysh is the symbol of a HEAD that brings to mind the IDEA of the head person or prince.

Reysh, the second letter in Berisheet, is also the number 200.

200 is the number that is used in the Bible to notify us as to the complete insufficiency of man. It is also a number that is often a prelude to an unexpected new event that declares the ALL sufficiency of God.

REYSH   BEYT

Pronounced **BAR**

Amazingly the first two letters in the word Berisheet is the Hebrew word for SON.

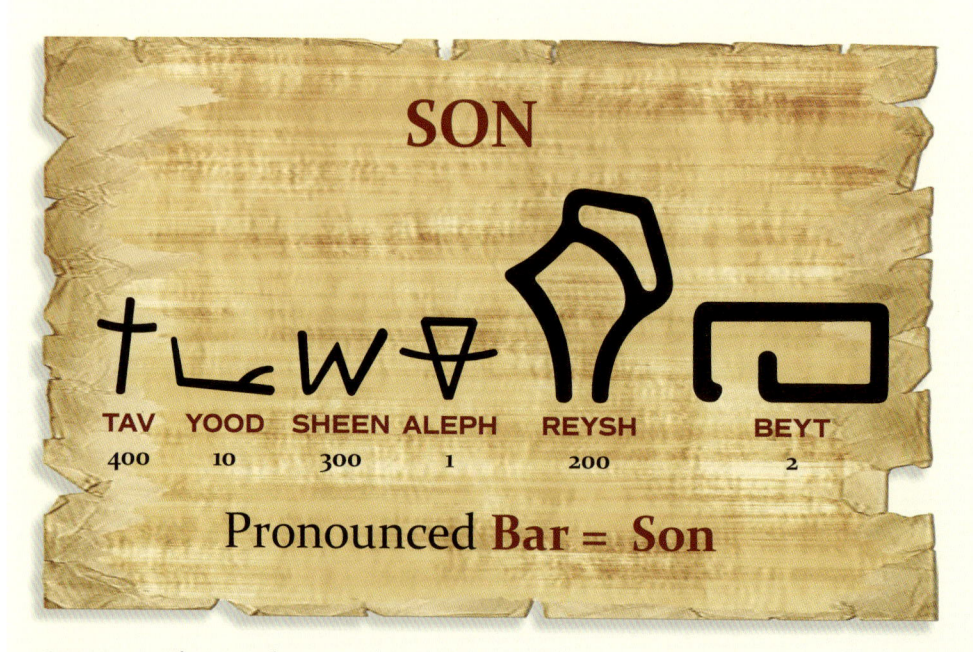

SON

TAV	YOOD	SHEEN	ALEPH	REYSH	BEYT
400	10	300	1	200	2

Pronounced **Bar = Son**

So, now we know who is in the tent.

He is someone's SON, who is also the head person or prince.

But Whose Son is He?

The third letter in Berisheet gives us the answer.

THE THIRD LETTER

TAV	YOOD	SHEEN	ALEPH	REYSH	BEYT
400	10	300	1	200	2

Aleph

ALEPH	-----	REYSH	BEYT
1		200	2

The THIRD Letter in BERISHEET is Aleph pictured as an OX.

Aleph is the symbol of the strong leader pictured as an OX.

Aleph is also the Number **1**.

It is not surprising that Aleph is the first letter in Elohim, the name of God first revealed in the Bible.

Aleph is a picture that is ideally meant to convey the IDEA of God the Father, the strong leader that guides and directs His family.

But wait, there is more.

When we add Aleph to the first two letters in Berisheet we discover another word.

The First Three Letters in **Berisheet** spell the Hebrew Word:

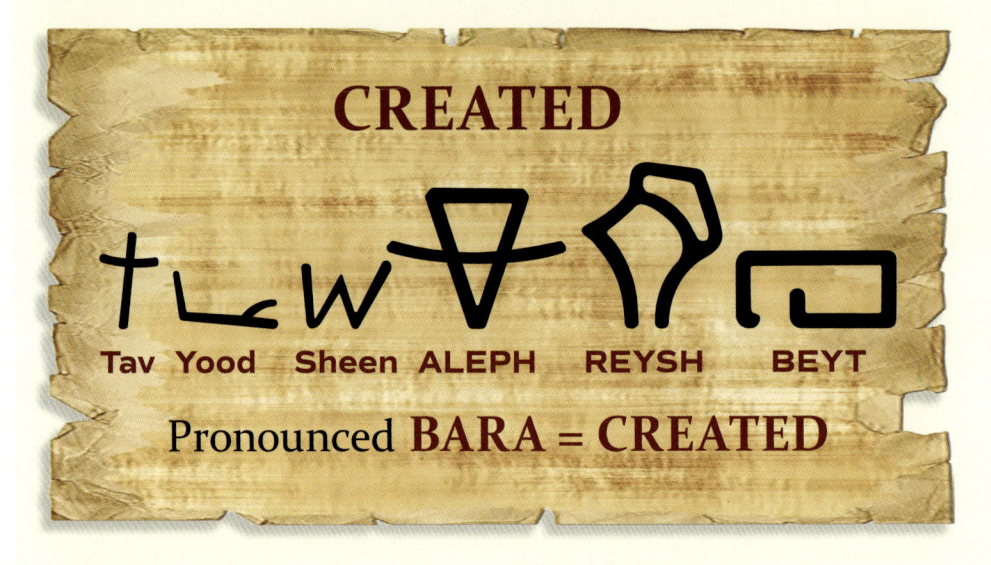

CREATED

Tav Yood Sheen ALEPH REYSH BEYT

Pronounced **BARA = CREATED**

Beyt Reysh Aleph, the first three Hebrew letters in Berisheet is also the Hebrew word for CREATED or CREATOR.

Who is in the Beyt or Tent?

The Beyt Reysh — **THE SON** — is in the Tent

Whose Son is HE?

He is the Beyt Reysh Aleph
THE SON OF GOD,

Who is also the Beyt Reysh Aleph
THE CREATOR.

THE FOURTH LETTER

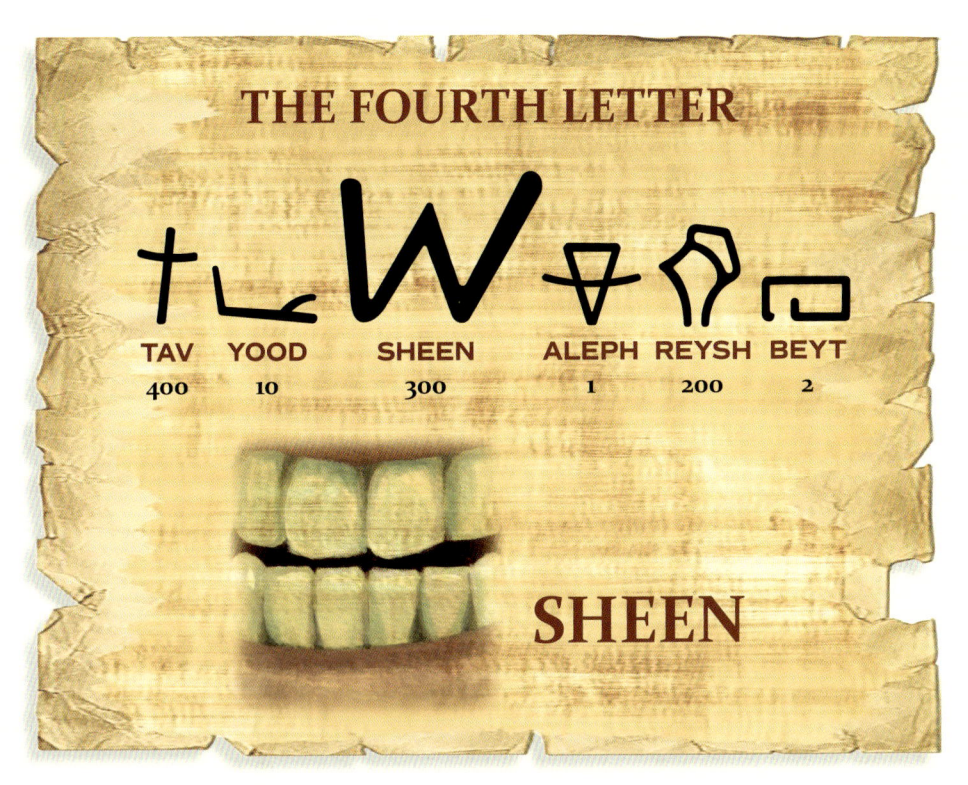

TAV	YOOD	SHEEN	ALEPH	REYSH	BEYT
400	10	300	1	200	2

SHEEN

Sheen, W the FOURTH letter in BERISHEET, is pictured as teeth.

Teeth press down, crush and destroy.

Sheen is also God's "signature" letter, the one letter that God uses to signify His special ownership of something.

Sheen is also the number 300.

300 is an amplification of the sacred number 3.

Three means DIVINE PERFECTION.

300 signifies a divinely–appointed blood sacrifice that results in victory over death.

Amazingly we find another Hebrew word nested in Berisheet.

Sheen, the fourth letter in Berisheet, is also the last letter in the Hebrew word Reysh.

The Second, Third and Fourth Letters in Berisheet spells the Hebrew Word for Head or First.

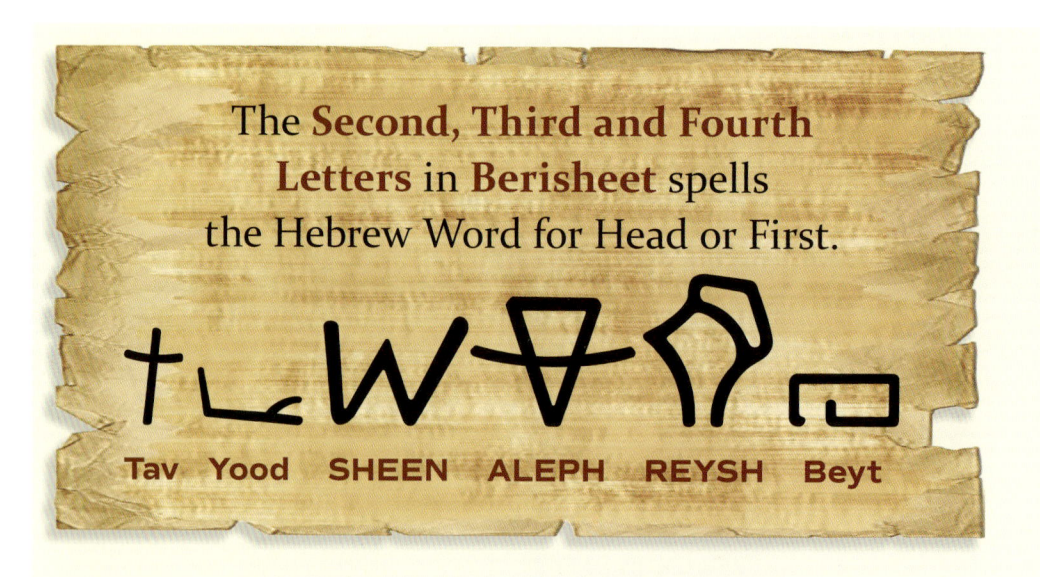

Tav Yood SHEEN ALEPH REYSH Beyt

Reysh is the Head Person, the Prince and the First.

NOTICE that the single Hebrew letter Reysh that is the second letter in Berisheet is also the three-letter Hebrew word Reysh spelled Reysh Aleph Sheen.

Reysh, the three-letter WORD, confirms the meaning of the single letter Reysh.

REYSH   BEYT

Pronounced **BAR**

To be clear, Reysh is not only the name of a letter it is also the word that means PRINCE or HEAD PERSON or FIRST in Hebrew.

Now I want to show you something that is very important.

Remember the Hebrew Word BAR translated as SON, the word that we found nested in the first two letters in Berisheet?

18 | THE BERISHEET END-TIMES PASSOVER PROPHECY
C.J. LOVIK

Notice that in the word Bar, the Reysh or Prince is INSIDE the Beyt.

With that in mind, we must ask why God put both the single letter Reysh and then nested the three-letter word Reysh in Berisheet.

Let me share at least one obvious reason.

The reason is that the LORD wanted us to know that the Reysh Aleph Sheen, the PRINCE, has come out of the tent.

The Prince has gone out of His HOME.

A picture is worth a thousand words.

The PRINCE who was INSIDE the house is now coming out of the house.

The SON Inside the HOUSE or TENT

REYSH   **BEYT**

Pronounced **BAR**

The PRINCE coming OUT of the House or Tent

SHEEN   **ALEPH**   **REYSH**   **BEYT**

Are you starting to understand how God communicates with His children?

For of such is the Kingdom of Heaven...our future Home!

Why is the PRINCE coming out of the tent?

The next three pictograms that compose the Hebrew word Berisheet give us the answer.

If Sheen W, the picture of teeth, means to crush and destroy, then we must ask: *Is the Son of God coming out of the tent to be crushed and destroyed* or is He coming out of His tent to crush and destroy?

OR Could it be BOTH?

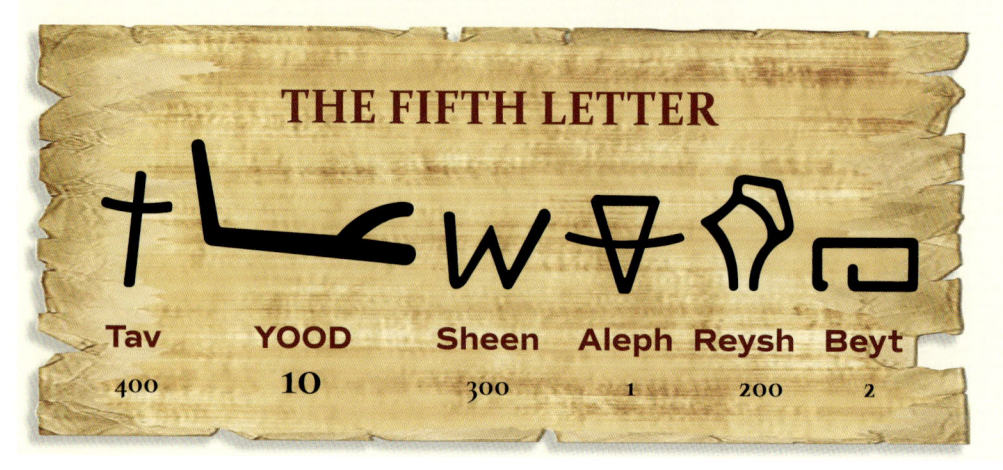

THE FIFTH LETTER

Tav	YOOD	Sheen	Aleph	Reysh	Beyt
400	10	300	1	200	2

THE BERISHEET END-TIMES PASSOVER PROPHECY
C.J. LOVIK

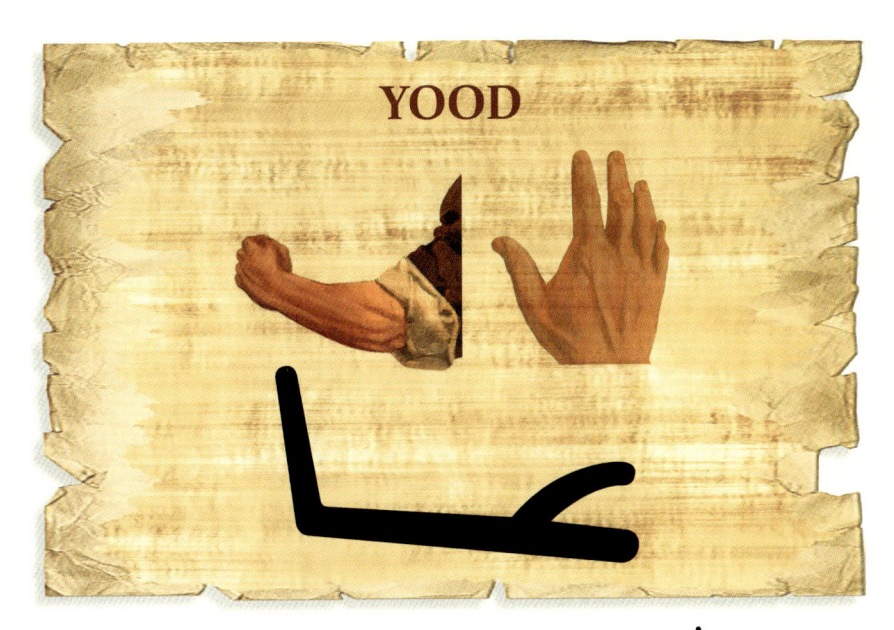

We will begin to unravel this mystery as we look at Yood, the fifth letter in Berisheet.

YOOD informs us that something amazing is going to unfold on the earth. Something that will MARK the END of one age and the BEGINNING of something new.

A new beginning!

We know this has something to do with the PRINCE coming out of His HOME in Heaven.

Yood is the 10th letter in the Hebrew Aleph-Beyt.

TEN is an important number because the primary meaning of the NUMBER 10 or YOOD gives added spiritual significance to the PICTURE YOOD, the hand doing a divine deed.

YOOD, the number 10, is one of FOUR sacred numbers and it means ORDINAL PERFECTION.

The picture of Yood, the hand or arm, informs us that God has ordained a PLAN in HEAVEN signified by Yood the number 10 that is going to unfold as a mighty deed that is accomplished on the earth.

Consider the number 10 for just a moment. Zero is not a number, in God's language, it is a placeholder for something else, and that something else is most often TIME.

So now we know why the PRINCE has come out of His heavenly home.

He is coming to earth to accomplish something His Heavenly Father planned and purposed in Heaven that will happen on the earth at the appointed TIME.

But What is that SOMETHING?

The answer is revealed in the final letter of Berisheet. Remember that Berisheet is the first word in the Bible. Notice that the last letter in Berisheet is TAV, the 22nd and final letter in the Hebrew Aleph-Beyt. Whatever this something is will bring an end to one thing as it begins another.

TAV, the FINAL letter in Berisheet, is pictured as a CROSS.

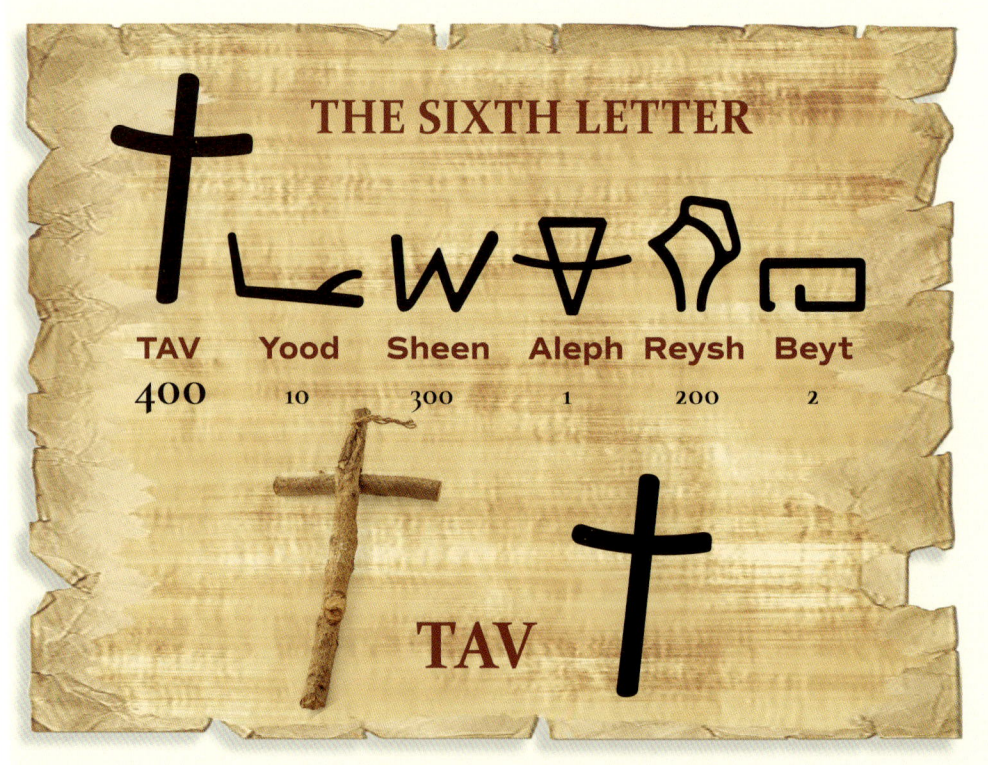

THE SIXTH LETTER

TAV	Yood	Sheen	Aleph	Reysh	Beyt
400	10	300	1	200	2

TAV

To be clear, the earliest Hebrew pictograms display this Hebrew symbol or letter as a cross. The pictogram displayed in this article is a faithful representation of the earliest Hebrew letter TAV pictured as a wooden cross.

Tav ✝, the last letter in the Berisheet prophecy, informs us that the divine deed ordained in Heaven ⌐10 will fulfill a covenant and be REVEALED as a sign that is literally pictured as a CROSS.

This SIGN will mark the center point for ALL human history from God's perspective!

Everything that happened before this SIGN ✝ was sovereignly ordained in order to set the stage for this ONE single event.

This is the one event that God considers the single MOST IMPORTANT event to happen on the earth and God has ordained it to happen at exactly the precise appointed time on His Seven-Thousand-Year calendar for mankind.

Everything that happens going forward from this sign ✝ is as a direct consequence of this epic event.

Whatever man may think is important pales in significance to what God thinks is important.

The CROSS ✝ MARKS the SPOT from which we can forecast every EPIC event that God has planned for Mankind in the future.

The SIGN

Is NOW History!

And the answer to why the PRINCE came out of His home in Glory has been revealed.

The Son of God left His home in Heaven to come to earth in order to accomplish His Heavenly Father's plan and purpose to redeem Mankind. This accomplishment took place on a crude wooden cross that lifted up the Son of God on a mount we know as Calvary.

This accomplishment reversed the Covenant that man had entered into with death and Hell and opened the door and fulfilled the covenant that God had made with His Son to redeem man and become the door that leads to the place that Jesus said He was going to prepare for all those that love and trust Him.

All those who have been redeemed by the atoning sacrifice of the perfect Lamb of God are now destined to enter God's HOME prepared by Yeshua for those He redeemed with His precious blood.

Berisheet is all about HOME and new beginnings.

The central beginning in view has now been revealed.

Has the Berisheet Prophecy been completely revealed and fulfilled?

> Yeshua Ha-Mashiach, the name of the Son of God, the Prince of Glory.

The answer is NOT EVEN CLOSE, the Berisheet Prophecy has only been partially revealed and has not yet been completely fulfilled.

So far, we have answered the question, "who?"

We have been introduced to the central Person in the Berisheet Prophecy. The central personality in all man's history. We now know the name of the Son of God, the Prince of Glory. His name is Yeshua Ha-Mashiach, Jesus the Christ.

Man, as a result of the sin of Adam and our own sin are in bondage to the CURSE of sin and under the WRATH of God. The Prince of Glory left His Heavenly home to atone for our sins so that we might be justified by His sacrifice and have eternal life and enter into the HOME that Jesus has gone to prepare for us.

Let's go on to discover the WHEN and WHERE that is revealed in the FINAL Berisheet Prophecy regarding the birth, death and resurrection of Yeshua.

You are about to discover the rest of the Berisheet Prophecy, including the timeline for the two most important events looming on the near horizon.

But before we continue, let's ask another question that begins with, "why."

Why has this prophecy been hidden for almost 3500 years? Why is it being revealed now, nearly 2000 years after the cross of Calvary?

Why NOW?

You will discover the answer to this important question in the next chapter of the Final Berisheet Prophecy. And the answer could well impact your eternity.

And if you want to know exactly where you are on God's 7000-year calendar, please continue reading.

CHAPTER 2

The Rapture and the Second Coming

BERISHEET "IN BEGINNING"

TAV	YOOD	SHEEN	ALEPH	REYSH	BEYT
400	10	300	1	200	2

The Berisheet Prophecy written 1500 years before the birth of the Messiah reveals what was on God's mind from the beginning. It is all about His Son.

We have already revealed the heroic narrative that is embedded in the six pictograms that prophetically illustrate the most important event to ever take place in the 6000 years of human history.

The Berisheet Prophecy reveals a pictographic narrative of the greatest beginning of all time. It is not the six-day creation that is in view but the beginning that ends man's covenant with sin and death and makes a way where there was no way.

The way that has been opened up for us to enter our HOME in Heaven. Opened by the only begotten Son of God who is the Prince of Glory. The Son of God who left His home in Heaven to come to earth as a servant in order to joyfully accomplish His Heavenly Father's plan and purpose to redeem fallen mankind in order that we might be invited into HIS HOME.

The Berisheet Prophecy notifies us that this divine deed would be accomplished on a wooden cross, and it reveals much, much more.

We are now ready to answer the two-remaining questions regarding the major prophetic theme that is highlighted in the very first word in the Bible.

WHEN AND WHERE?

When will the epic event take place and where on earth is it this going to happen?

Does the Berisheet Prophecy reveal WHERE this epic blood sacrifice that atoned for the sins of fallen man would take place?

The answer can be found in the Hebrew letter SHEEN, the fourth Hebrew letter in Berisheet.

The letter Sheen, as we learned, signifies pressing, gnashing and destruction.

Sheen is also the number 300.

The number 300 (Sheen) is used in connection with Enoch, Noah, Gideon, Sampson, David and Jesus to signify a supernatural victory over death.

Was there a "crushing" that took place before the supernatural victory over death?

If you have read any one of the four Gospel accounts, then you know the answer to this question.

To discover more about Sheen the number 300 we invite you to visit **PassoverProphecy.com.**

Sheen is also the one letter that is the shorthand signature of God's name. A name that signifies divine ownership.

Not all was a loss in Babylon, however. Take a look at the letter Sheen as it looks today in Modern Hebrew.

ש

A picture is worth a thousand words.

2 CHRONICLES 6:6A
But I have chosen Jerusalem, that my name might be there;

2 CHRONICLES 33:7
...In this house, and in Jerusalem, which I have chosen before all the tribes of Israel, will I put my name for ever:

Notice below that all three valleys that form the three fingers of Sheen all begin at Mount Moriah. The very SPOT where the Messiah offered Himself up for the sins of man. The very spot where God said He would write His name.

Included below is an ancient map of Jerusalem.

Notice that there are three valleys that come together at the base of Mount Moriah.

The Kidron Valley on the right, the Central Valley in the middle and the Hinnom Valley on the left.

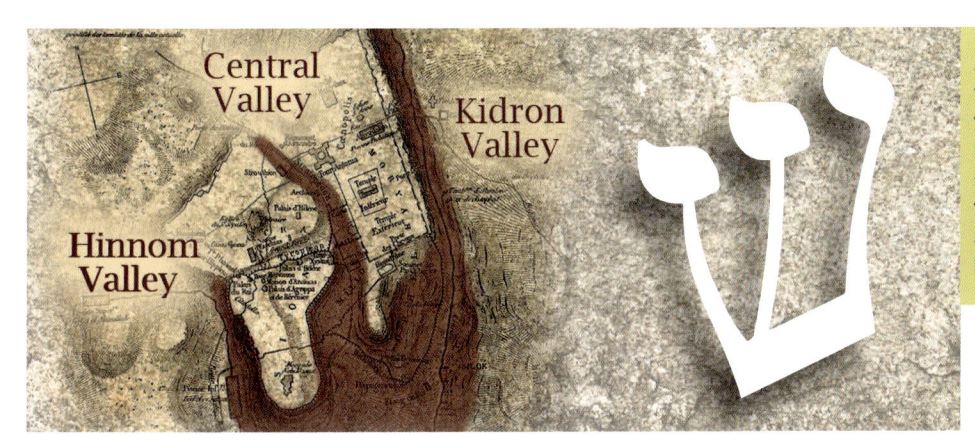

Jerusalem map with the valleys that surround it. Note the similarity with the letter Sheen as it looks today.

So in summary, the answer is YES, the Berisheet End-Times Passover Prophecy reveals the very spot that God ordained in Heaven in order to accomplish His grand purpose to redeem fallen man.

Mount Moriah, the place Christians call Calvary, marks the spot where the Berisheet prophecy would take place.

The final question is WHEN will this happen?

Does the Berisheet prophecy reveal WHEN the epic event on Mount Moriah would take place?

If so, where would we look for this clue?

The TIME-STAMP found in the Yood and Tav, the last two Hebrew Numbers revealed in Berisheet, gives us the answer.

The two letters directly connect the Sign of the Wooden Cross with the revelation that this sign is going to manifest itself at exactly the right time, a time appointed in Heaven before the foundation of the earth.

The same two letters or pictograms that revealed WHY the Son of God was coming out of His home in Glory also literally reveals the ultimate SIGN OF THE TIMES.

The same two pictograms that combine the idea of a plan ordained in Heaven that is going to unfold on the earth at the appointed time points us to the picture of the covenant and the Sign of the Wooden Cross.

The number Yood or TEN is the key that unlocks the mystery of WHEN this is all going to take place.

Yood is often used as God's divine multiplier.

Yood often reveals that events will unfold on earth at the time appointed in Heaven.

The Berisheet time stamp prophecy is very simple to understand and needs little explanation.

COVENANT • Ordinal Perfection - a Divine Deed
SIGN • Ordained in Heaven and Accomplished
CROSS • On the earth at the Appointed Time

400 X 10 = 4000 YEARS

The Tav and the Yood provide the answer.

400 x 10 equals exactly 4000 years!

Before we continue I need to address the question of dating the death of Jesus. This is a topic that has been debated for the last 100 years. Tradition in today's church teaches that Jesus died in the year 33 AD.

Many of the early first and second-century church fathers taught that Jesus died in 30 AD, a belief that exists among most biblical literalist to this day.

Since, as you are about to discover, the date that Jesus died on the cross of Calvary is not only the center-point of all man's history, it may also be the date from which all the other major events from God's perspective find their starting point. Are all the big events from the creation account found in Genesis to the New Heavens and New Earth forecast in the book of Revelation scheduled on God's time-table based on the cross event? After you finish reading this book, I believe you will agree that the answer is a resounding YES!

So, when did Jesus die on the Cross?

If we were to ask a hundred bible scholars that question, we would get a half-dozen definitive answers ranging from 28 AD to 33 AD.

Whatever position we take on the question of Jesus' death date is likely to raise the alarm with many of our readers. Since all the time span prophecies in this book are based on the date that Jesus died on the cross, and since there is no agreed upon date, we have decided to pick a date that splits the difference. We will use a date between those that hold an early 28 AD date, and those that believe in the 33 AD date promoted by church tradition.

To be clear, this book is not designed to settle the argument about when Jesus

The Crucifixion of the Parlement of Paris, unknown author, Circa 1452.

died on the cross, but rather to present an ancient prophetic perspective that we believe has, at its start-point, the date Jesus died on the cross.

The good news is that almost everyone agrees that Jesus died somewhere between 28 AD and 33 AD. So, we will leave it to those that believe Jesus died in 33 AD to ADD three years to all the proposed time-stamp prophecies presented for your consideration in this book. Likewise, to those that believe Jesus died in 28 AD (a date that resonates with me personally), simply SUBTRACT two years from the time line prophecies.

For the purpose of displaying the Millennial Sabbath End Times Perspective, we will arbitrarily select the year 30 AD in hopes that everyone understands that we are not trying to unravel the mystery of the date of Christ's death. Rather, we are attempting to reveal a time-stamp prophecy found in the first book of the Bible, pinpointed to within a half-decade, depending upon your own personal convictions regarding the date of the death of Jesus the Christ.

Adoration of the Shepherds by the Dutch painter Gerard van Honthorst, 1622.

Obviously, with this in mind, no one can accuse us of date-setting, as we are presenting a perspective that is the oldest and most revered eschatology on the earth. Of course, we are talking about the Millennial thousand-year-for-a-day end times perspective.

So, let's go back to the Yood and the Tav that gives us the first time-frame prophetic marker in the Berisheet prophecy.

A prophetic time stamp of 4000 years.

Keep in mind that we are looking at the Berisheet Prophecy through the lens of the end-times prophetic perspective that is based on the belief that God has communicated in both pattern and type and by direct revelation that He has allotted 7000 years for mankind on the present earth. This perspective is called the Millennial Day or the Sabbath Millennial Day or Day for a Thousand-years perspective. Remember that his method of calculating the unfolding of time, whatever name you prefer to call it, is the oldest prophetic Biblical perspective on the earth.

Does that make it right?

No, but it certainly makes it something worth considering.

The Millennial day for a thousand-year concept is very simple and easy to grasp.

GOD gave mankind from the very beginning a 7-literal-days repeating cycle.

God then revealed that from HIS PERSPECTIVE that each literal creation day was as a 1000-years and a 1000-years as one day from HIS DIVINE PERSPECTIVE.

Leaving us in no doubt as to what He had on His mind, He further revealed in His word the importance of the number 7.

Throughout the Bible, the number 7, considered a sacred number, meant DIVINE COMPLETION.

The basic concept is that God has given Man six thousand years to work. That work will cease at the end of 6000 years to be followed by one thousand years of REST.

So, in a nutshell, the 7000-year millennial perspective believes that the age of mankind started with the year of creation, unfolds for 6000 years of labor, and ends with the last 1000 years of rest.

So now the question is *does the Berisheet YOOD TAV Prophecy reveal the **precise** year when the crucifixion of Jesus would take place?*

Are there **exactly** 4000 years between creation and the cross of Calvary?

If you believe in the Millennial Day for a thousand-years perspective you might say YES, the time prophecy is close enough.

After all, if Jesus died on the cross in 30 AD and the prophecy predicts that the Cross Event is going to happen 4000 years starting from the Creation date of approximately 4004 BC then that is close enough. Right?

The problem is that when you do the math starting with the Creation date for 4004 BC and going forward 4000 years you're left with an extra 33-33.5 years.

For some, that is close enough. But for those that take God's word literally, it is a real problem.

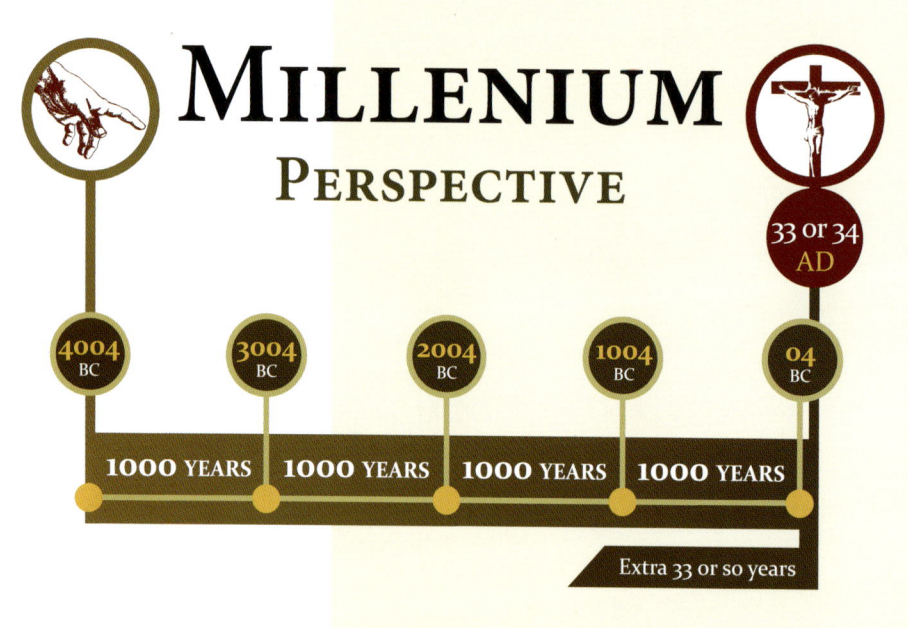

Millenium
Perspective

4004 BC — 1000 YEARS — **3004 BC** — 1000 YEARS — **2004 BC** — 1000 YEARS — **1004 BC** — 1000 YEARS — **04 BC** — **33 or 34 AD**

Extra 33 or so years

With the perspective that missing the mark by only 33 years is close enough, it would be impossible to predict the future events on God's Millennial Calendar with any precision. If a thousand years is no longer a literal time span but simply a rough estimate then the Millennial Day for a thousand-years perspective is no longer a prophecy but simply a concept in which precision is not the object of the revelation.

Is there evidence in the Bible, based on prophetic times revealed as harbingers of future events, that would warrant this sort of variation and imprecision when it comes to God's revelations regarding when something is going to take place?

In other words, when God says a thousand years can we take Him seriously and literally or are we just to take it as an approximation?

So, let's ask the question again.

Does the Berisheet Yood Tav time-stamp prophecy reveal the exact precise year when the crucifixion of Jesus would take place starting from the 4004 BC year of creation and going forward 4000 years?

The answer is NO.

NOW, let's look at this from another perspective.

Let's consider that God in His great wisdom DID NOT provide us the exact year of the crucifixion year starting with a countdown from creation.

Instead, God provided us with something much more amazing.

God provided us with a measuring rod that reveals time in 1000-year increments, a millennial view that is designed to take us right back to the first chapter in Genesis where we are meant to consider again the meaning of the six days of creation.

Six days of labor followed by the 7th day of rest.

Do you see the prophetic pattern that forecasts the millennial reign of Messiah in every cycle of the six days of creation followed by the seventh day of rest?

Notice the weekly pattern that God designed to repeat hundreds of thousands of time as both a rehearsal and a prophetic harbinger that heralds the final 7th day.

Is this a foreshadowing of the one-thousand-year millennial reign of God's Son on the earth?

God has provided us a Millennial-Time-Span that is complimentary and consistent with the 6-days for a thousand-year pattern God set forth as a pattern in Genesis 1.

Consider that the "1 day with the Lord is as a 1000-years" revelation revealed in both the Old and New Testament gives us a divine perspective that is ultimately confirmed by the LORD JESUS Himself. Jesus reveals this time perspective six times in the book of Revelation. Is it a coincidence that six thousand years is the exact time period that must end before He inaugurates His 7th-day up-coming Kingly reign on the earth?

The seventh day, the final day that will last exactly 1000-years.

If the seventh day is exactly a thousand-years, then the other 6 days must also be precisely a thousand-years each.

Six days equals exactly 6000 years.

This is the foundational numeric concept that fueled the Sabbath Millennial End Times Perspective, the oldest eschatology in the world.

This is a prophetic viewpoint held by both the ancient Jewish Rabbis and the early church fathers.

The Millennial Perspective is now out of favor with the biblical literalist because it seems to have failed.

Many Christians who believed that the millennial-day-for-a-thousand-years perspective calculated from the START DATE of Creation in 4004 BC would climax in the second coming of Christ in the years leading up to the year 2000 AD.

It would be prudent to highlight that many Christians today cannot distinguish between the Second Coming of Christ and the Rapture of the Church. They are, in fact, two separate events. The Rapture is a departure of the Church and is a sign-less event. The Second Coming is an event which will result in a culmination or conclusion of all things here on earth.

Below is a chart comparing these two events in Scripture. Many people have a tendency to combine these two events, but if you read Scripture carefully, you will see that either a) there are several contradicting passages regarding a single event, or b) there are two events. Obviously, we hold to the inerrancy of Scripture, and thus option b is the only valid choice.

Many are confused about the two-stage coming of Jesus in the last days just as they were confused about His first coming. God has a wonderful purpose that is gloriously displayed in His plans as they unfold on the earth.

The following is meant to help those who still may be confused about the Second Coming and the Blessed Hope.

Misunderstanding abounds in these final days as Satan is stirring the pot of chaos and confusion in order to remove Christians from the wonderful promises made to them as members of the mystery church that has been revealed in the last days.

Titus 2:13

Looking for that blessed hope, and the glorious appearing of the great God and our Savior Jesus Christ;

Is investigating prophecy discouraged in the Scripture?

Matthew 24:34-36

Verily I say unto you, This generation shall not pass, till all these things be fulfilled. Heaven and earth shall pass away, but my words shall not pass away. But of that day and hour knoweth no man, no, not the angels of Heaven, but my Father only.

If you read Matthew 24, you will not come away with the idea that Jesus is telling His disciples that His second coming is a forbidden topic. On the contrary, Jesus is encouraging them to observe the signs and be prepared for His return.

This is the most subscribed to and enduring end-times perspective held by both Jews and Gentiles. This is the end-times eschatology and has been taught as an end-times outlook for over 3000 years.

THE RAPTURE / DEPARTURE OF THE CHURCH
THE SECOND COMING OF JESUS CHRIST

Who Goes and Who Stays?

The Rapture / Departure of the Church
Removes all Believers from the earth.
1 Thessalonians 4:13-18
1 Corinthians 15:50-54

The Second Coming of Jesus Christ
will result in the Removal of All Unbelievers from the earth.
Matthew 24:37-41

Observation:

If believers remain on the earth as recorded in **Matthew 25:34** and unbelievers are removed as recorded in **Matthew 24:37-41**, we are left with a contradiction.
The solution is simple. We are investigating two similar but separate events that happen at different times in order to accomplish altogether different purposes.

Who Comes and Who Goes?

In **the Rapture / Departure of the Church** Christ comes FOR His OWN.
John 14:3
1 Thessalonians 4:14
2 Thessalonians 2:1

The Second Coming of Jesus Christ comes WITH His OWN.
1 Thessalonians 3:13
Jude 1:14
Revelation 19:14-16

In Other Words...

In **the Rapture / Departure of the Church** Christ Comes to Collect His BRIDE from the earth.
1 Thessalonians 4:16-17

In **the Second Coming of Jesus Christ** Comes with His BRIDE back to earth.
Revelation 19:14-16

The Father's House

After **the Rapture / Departure of the Church** Those who belong to Christ will be taken To the Father's House.
1 Thessalonians 4:16-17

In **the Second Coming of Jesus Christ** Those saved out of the Great Tribulation Will Not See the Father's House.
Revelation 20:4-5

THE BERISHEET END-TIMES PASSOVER PROPHECY
C.J. LOVIK

THE RAPTURE / DEPARTURE OF THE CHURCH	THE SECOND COMING OF JESUS CHRIST
Who is it ALL ABOUT?	
After **the Rapture / Departure of the Church** The focus and object of attention is the Lord's Church. *1 Thessalonians 4:15-17*	**The Second Coming of Jesus Christ** focuses all the attention on Israel and the Kingdom. *Matthew 24:14*
What is the Location of Christ's Coming?	
The Rapture / Departure of the Church Christ comes in the clouds and believers meet Jesus in the air. *1 Thessalonians 4:17*	In the **Second Coming of Jesus** Christ Comes to the earth where He sets His feet on solid ground. *Zechariah 14:4* *Acts 1:11*
What Happens Next?	
After **the Rapture / Departure of the Church** The next prophetic event is The Great Tribulation. *2 Thessalonians 1:6-9*	After the **Second Coming of Jesus Christ** The next event is the establishment of the Millennial Kingdom here on the earth. *Revelation 20:7-8*
Signs or No Signs?	
No Signs Precede **the Rapture / Departure of the Church.** The Rapture could happen at any time before the Day of the Lord. *1 Thessalonians 5:1-3*	Many Signs Precede **the Second Coming of Jesus Christ.** *Luke 21:11* *Luke 21:15*

THE BERISHEET END-TIMES PASSOVER PROPHECY
CHAPTER 2: THE RAPTURE AND THE SECOND COMING

THE RAPTURE / DEPARTURE OF THE CHURCH	THE SECOND COMING OF JESUS CHRIST
What Happens After Jesus Comes?	
After **the Rapture / Departure of the Church** Jesus will gather His bride to Himself in preparation for The Marriage of the Lamb. *Revelation 19:6-9*	After the **Second Coming Jesus** Christ will execute judgment on the earth and establish His Kingdom. *Zechariah 14:3-4* *Jude 14-15* *Revelation 19:11-21*
How Quickly Does Jesus Come?	
The Rapture / Departure of the Church happens in a moment, In the Twinkling of an Eye. Only believers will see the Lord after the living and the dead have been glorified and translated. Those that died in Christ will return with Him in their spirit bodies and will precede the living in being clothed with immortal glorified bodies. *1 Corinthians 15:52*	**The Second coming of Jesus Christ** is Slow in coming by comparison. Everyone will see Jesus coming with great power and authority. It does not happen in one instant of time. *Zechariah 12:10* *Matthew 24:30* *Revelation 1:7*
What about the Resurrection of the Dead?	
The Rapture / Departure of the Church includes the glorious Resurrection of the "Dead in Christ" along with the translation of the living. *1 Thessalonians 4:13-18* *1 Corinthians 15:51-54*	**The Second Coming of Jesus** makes no reference to a resurrection. *Zechariah 12:10* *Zechariah 14:4-5* *Revelation 1:7, 19:11-21*

THE RAPTURE / DEPARTURE OF THE CHURCH

THE SECOND COMING OF JESUS CHRIST

What about the Angels?

The Rapture / Departure of the Church
Angels do not come to gather the Church.
Matthew 24:31
2 Thessalonians 1:7-10

During the Second Coming of Jesus
Angels come to gather and transport Jews from the four corners of the earth to Israel.
Matthew 13:39, 41&49
Matthew 24:31

What about Glorified Resurrection Bodies?

In the Rapture / Departure of the Church, those who have died in Christ will return with Jesus with their spirit bodies to receive their Glorified Resurrection Bodies.
1 Thessalonians 4:17

At the **Second Coming of Jesus,** Christians will return to the earth with Christ having already been given a resurrected body and riding on white horses.
Revelation 19:11

Where is the White Horse?

In the Rapture / Departure of the Church, Jesus returns and is NOT riding a white horse.

After the **Second Coming of Jesus Christ** He will return riding a white horse.
Revelation 19:11

Good News or Bad News? Which is it?

In the Rapture / Departure of the Church. Jesus comes with a message of hope and comfort.
1 Thessalonians 4:18
Titus 2:13
1 John 3:3

At **the Second Coming,** Jesus comes with a message of judgment
Joel 3:12-16
Malachi 4:5
Revelation 20:1-2

THE RAPTURE / DEPARTURE OF THE CHURCH | THE SECOND COMING OF JESUS CHRIST

What about Satan?

In the Rapture / Departure of the Church the world is found in a state of Satanic deception.
2 Thessalonians 2:3-12

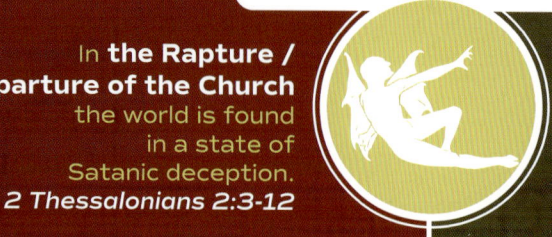

At the Second Coming of Jesus Satan is bound.
Revelation 20:1-2

Who Sees Christ and Who Doesn't?

In the Rapture / Departure of the Church, only believers alive on the Earth will see the Lord Jesus coming! No one else will see Him.
1 Thessalonians 4:17

At the Second Coming of Jesus, all will see Jesus descend bodily and visibly.
Acts 1:9-11

What about the Judgments?

The Rapture / Departure of the Church, followed by the Bema seat (rewards) judgment seat of Christ.
2 Corinthians 5:9-11

The Second Coming of Jesus will be followed by the Judgment of the nations.
Matthew 24:32-46

What kind of bodies will we have?

In the Rapture / Departure of the Church. the Saints will receive a New Immortal glorified body that is like the body of Jesus.
Philippians 3:21
1 Corinthians 15:51-54

At the Second Coming of Jesus the Tribulation Saints will enter the Millennium with their earthly bodies.
Isaiah 65:20

THE BERISHEET END-TIMES PASSOVER PROPHECY
C.J. LOVIK

THE RAPTURE / DEPARTURE OF THE CHURCH
THE SECOND COMING OF JESUS CHRIST

What about the Antichrist?

After **the Rapture / Departure of the Church** the Antichrist will be revealed and given a period of time to deceive the entire world.

2 Thessalonians 2:8

At the **Second Coming of Jesus** the Antichrist is defeated and cast into the lake of fire.

Revelation 19:20

What about Israel?

After **the Rapture / Departure of the Church,** Israel is persecuted with two out of every three Jews perishing in the terrible time of Jacob's trouble.

Zechariah 13:8-9

At the **Second Coming of Jesus** Israel is gathered and established as the head of the nations.

Jeremiah 23:5-8

What about the New World Order?

After **the Rapture / Departure of the Church,** The New World Order is the dominant world government. The world will be plagued by famine, pestilence, war, and other sorrows too numerous to mention.

Revelation 13:15
Matthew 24:6-10
Luke 17:31

After the **Second Coming of Jesus** The Kingdom of Jesus is established in Jerusalem where He reigns on the earth for 1000-years ushering in true peace and security.

Isaiah 11:6
Daniel 2:34-35

THE BERISHEET END-TIMES PASSOVER PROPHECY
CHAPTER 2: THE RAPTURE AND THE SECOND COMING

When the return of Christ did not happen in 2000 AD, many Christians lost confidence in the accuracy of the millennial day for a thousand-years perspective.

It seems that the Millennial time clock is not as precise as some had imagined.

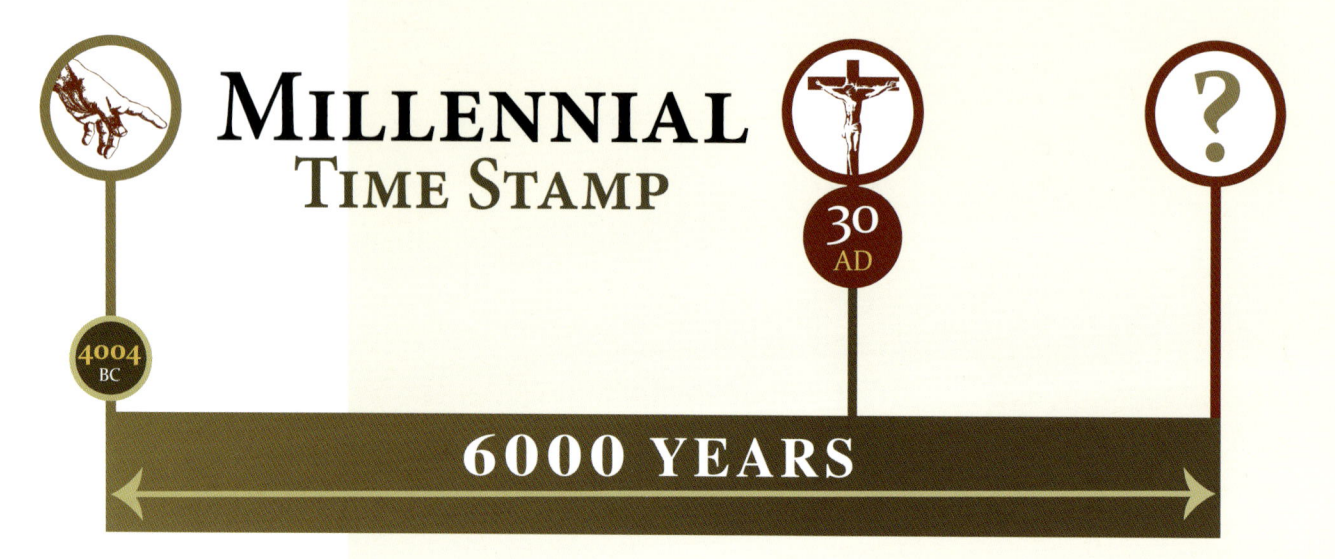

Millennial Time Stamp

4004 BC — **6000 YEARS** — **30 AD** — **?**

Obviously, God has not failed.

Perhaps the day for a thousand-years is, after all, just an approximation and not to be taken literally.

Should we just admit that the day for a thousand-year millennial perspective failed?

Or, has man failed to understand it from God's vantage point?

Let God be true, and every man a liar! Remember that the foolishness of God is wiser than men; and the weakness of God is stronger than men, and His ways are not our ways...shall I go on?

Let's take a look at this from another point of view.

Let's take a fresh look at this asking two questions.

When did the Son of God die on the cross?

Why did the Son of God die on the cross?

In other words, when did the sign in the Yood & Tav, the last two letters in the Berisheet prophecy take place?

Why did the Savior hang on the Cross of Calvary in 30 AD?

He died to reverse the curse that Adam and all his descendants, including you and me, are now under.

He died as an atonement for the sin and rebelliousness of Adam and all his descendants including you and me.

With the **When** and the **Why** fresh in our minds, let's look one more time at the 4000-year Time-Stamp measuring rod that allows us to look back in time starting from the Crucifixion of Christ on Passover in 30 AD.

But instead of going forward from the proposed start-date of Creation, what happens when we look back in time 4000 years from the Cross of Calvary?

> As we have already established, we will be using 30 AD as the date of the cross event.

Will we discover that the Millennial Time Stamp of 4000 years is an approximation based on the start-date of Creation or will we discover the reason, precision and majesty of this millennial prophetic time-stamp from God's point of view?

When we take this 4000-year measuring rod and lay it on the time line starting on Passover in 30 AD and go back in time 4000 years, what event do we discover?

We discover a date that no one has considered up until now.

THE BERISHEET END-TIMES PASSOVER PROPHECY
CHAPTER 2: THE RAPTURE AND THE SECOND COMING

We discover a year whose monumental spiritual significance has been hidden for over 6000 years.

We discover the year 3970 BC (based on the proposed 30 AD cross event).

Why is this year important?

Since 3970 BC is obviously not the date of Creation based on biblical chronology why is this date important?

Let's look at this again adding the missing puzzle piece.

If we start at the CROSS, on Passover in 30 AD, and go back in time 4000 years it takes us to the year 3970 BC.

If we then start with the year 3970 BC and we go back in time another **33 - 33.5** years what date do land on?

The answer is 4004 BC, but could be 4001-4006 BC depending on the cross event timing.

What is important about the year 4004 BC?

The 'Berisheet' PASSOVER Prophecy
Pattern is Prophecy

3966 YRS.

CREATION 4004 BC — 33+ YEARS — FIRST ADAM SINS 3970 BC

33+ YEARS — LAST ADAM SAVES 30 AD PASSOVER — 04 BC

4004 BC is one of the dates believed by many students of biblical chronology to be the most reliable year to date the Creation.

Just to be perfectly clear, the Creation date of approximately 4004 BC is based on a literal interpretation of the Bible and the chronologies revealed in the sacred Word of God.

Bishop Ussher is not the only Bible scholar that believed that Creation took place in 4004 BC.

Did you notice that I did not start this prophetic forecast from the proposed starting point of Creation in 4004 BC and go forward in time?

NO.

I arrived at the 4004 BC date by taking Berisheet End-Times Passover Prophecy literally and then looking back in history 4000 years and finally adding 33-33.5 years to the equation.

Are you wondering why I added 33-33.5 years to the 4000-year forecast?

33-33.5 years is the number of years Jesus was on the earth, from His birth to His resurrection and ascension.

Bishop James Ussher, painting by Sir Peter Lely, 1680

Pattern is Prophecy!

If Pattern is Prophecy then it is only reasonable to expect that the 33-33.5 years of the sinless life of the Last Adam, whose name is Jesus the Christ, would match up exactly with the sinless life of the first Adam in the Garden of Eden during the very brief age of innocence.

We can reasonably surmise that the first Adam lived 33-33.5 sinless years in the Garden of Eden before he spiritually died, the moment he sinned.

The garden of Eden with the fall of man, (painting detail). artists Jan Brueghel de Oude and Peter Paul Rubens, 1615.

Adam's sin resulted in immediate spiritual death and the onset of decay that would result in his physical death at 930 years old.

The sinful act of Adam resulted in death and corruption to all his descendants including you and me.

Let's take a moment to consider the "day" Adam died.

Has God also clued us in to the one day is as a 1000-year concept revealed by both the six-day Creation account and the physical death of Adam? Consider that God told Adam that he would die the day he ate the forbidden fruit, and yet Adam lived to be 930 years old.

Was God notifying us to His prophetic concept of a day being as a 1000-years in His sight? Did Adam, according to God's prophetic way of reckoning, physically die on the very day he ate the forbidden fruit, a day being on God's calendar as a 1000-years?

Now let's consider the 33-33.5 years of our Lord's life here on the earth.

Is it really that surprising that the pattern set by the first Adam in the Garden would be duplicated with precision by the last Adam, Jesus Christ, who came to reverse the curse set in motion by the first Adam?

Clearly, Jesus was 33-33.5 years old when He died on the cross on Passover in 30 AD. That is a historical fact.

Now notice that the Berisheet Prophecy does not send us back to the date of Creation, it sends us back to the precise moment that sin entered into the heart of the First Adam.

Now we know why the year 3970 BC is important!

The year 3970 BC is most likely the year that SIN entered the world.

If you allow that it was 33-33.5 years from the Creation of Adam to the moment he sinned and then add the 3970 years forecast by the going back in time 4000 from the crucifixion of Christ, what date do you land on?

When did the countdown of 4000 years begin?

From Creation?

From the moment Adam sinned?

When did God start the countdown of 4000 years that would climax in the sacrifice that would cancel the covenant with sin and death that Adam and all his descendants have entered into?

Also, notice that if Jesus died on the Cross on Passover in 30 AD at the age of 33-33.5, then by going back in time 33-33.5 years in time we can determine that Jesus was born in 4-5 BC.

Recall that 4-5 BC date is a commonly agreed upon date for the birth of Jesus.

The Berisheet End-Times Passover Prophecy

Pattern is Prophecy

CREATION 4004 BC — 33+ YEARS — **FIRST ADAM SINS 3970 BC** — **3966 YRS.** — **LAST ADAM BORN 04 BC** — 33+ YEARS — **LAST ADAM SAVES 30 AD PASSOVER**

When we go back in time 4000 years from the birth of Jesus in 4 BC, we are back to the Creation date of 4004 BC, the most likely date of Creation.

Are you beginning to see the perfect time pattern that overlays the sinless life of the first Adam in the Garden of Eden that ended in rebellion and sin after 33-33.5 years in the Garden of Eden?

Can you now see the pattern repeated in order to accomplish the cancellation of the sin debt caused by the sin of the first Adam? This debt was canceled by the sinless life, death and resurrection of the Last Adam who died on a cross in 30 AD exactly 4000 years from the moment sin entered into the world of man?

Prophecy is pattern!

Until the Berisheet PASSOVER event unfolded in time and space in 30 AD, the Berisheet prophecy could not have been understood.

The logic of this is seamless, simple and profound.

Sinless Adam did not need a Savior for the first 33-33.5 sinless years of his life in the Garden of Eden.

But the dreadful moment Adam sinned at the age of 33-33.5 years old he had a desperate need for a Savior.

God is very precise in His dealings with man.

Consider the precision and accuracy of the Berisheet End-Times Passover Prophecy.

God began the prophetic countdown to the most important event to ever happen in human history; the exact moment that marked the desperate need for Redemption and Atonement.

That countdown started the clock ticking that would announce the coming Savior. That countdown started exactly 33-33.5 years AFTER Creation and is the starting point for the Millennial Sabbath End-Times Prophetic Perspective.

Adam and Eve Are Driven out of Eden, Gustave Doré, Doré's English Bible, 1866.

Amazingly, the Berisheet Prophecy revealed that we needed to reset the millennial perspective to the correct start date that up until now has been a mystery.

The year that sin entered the world 33-33.5 years after Creation can now be marked with a big black **X**.

I believe this marks the starting point for the 4000-year countdown to the cross and resets the Sabbath Millennial Calendar to the correct starting point.

Does this begin to satisfy the **Isaiah 46:9-10 prophecy?**

> *Remember the former things of old:*
>
> *for I am God, and there is none else;*
>
> *I am God, and there is none like me,*
>
> ## *Declaring the end from the beginning,*
>
> *and from ancient times the things that are not yet done, saying,*
>
> *My counsel shall stand, and I will do all my pleasure:*

Have we discovered the END God spoke about through His prophet Isaiah?

The answer is NO, the Cross is not the end of the Prophecy, it is the most amazing of all new beginnings.

There are two more time-stamped events yet to be revealed in the prophecy that we call the Berisheet End-Times Passover Prophecy that was fulfilled in 30 AD on a wooden cross.

The Berisheet End-Times Passover Prophecy reveals two more events that will satisfy Isaiah's prophecy and give us hope that the Sabbath Millennial End-Times perspective has not failed, but is on the cusp of unfolding in our generation.

When these events unfold in rapid succession, your future will either be bright and unimaginably hopeful or it will be filled with unspeakable terror.

What does your future hold?

Will you be ready and waiting for your Lord's return or will you be SO suffocated by the cares of this world that you cannot be bothered to wake up and look up?

I invite you to consider the final Berisheet End-Times Passover Prophecy.

The end is nearer than you ever imagined.

The Blessed Hope for some, the advent of terror for others.

Where are we on God's Millennial Countdown?

CHAPTER 3

The Berisheet
End-Times Passover Prophecy

In the first word in the Bible we have discovered the very first prophecy in the Bible. This prophetic revelation discloses, to our amazement, the central thematic event of all history, from God's point of view.

In the very first word in the Bible, we have discovered the vantage point from which, for the first time, we can correctly overlay the Sabbath Millennial End-Times perspective that God revealed to anyone paying attention to the Prophetic patterns and types that are the bedrock of all prophecy.

For thousands of years there has been one Biblical prophetic perspective has been obvious but blurred and out of focus, missing the final lens that, once in place, would bring the entire vista into sharp perspective.

There is just one puzzle piece that has been hidden in place from the very beginning just waiting for the appointed time to be put into the right place in order that the terminal generation might view it at the appointed time just before God ends one age and begins another.

The millennial historical time-span-perspective that is now in focus reveals for the first time when the most important events, the events that changed the course or man's history, took place in the past.

It accomplishes this NOT by going forward from the proposed year of the six-day Creation account but, by looking back to the year of Creation and the events that immediately followed the placement of Adam and Eve in the Garden of Eden.

The 7000-year millennial perspective, as it turns out, is filled with the unfolding of many dispensations over time but only ONE CONDITION and one beginning and ending that is in view from a divine perspective.

And what condition is that?

The condition of man's heart, the condition of sin and rebellion.

The 7000-year countdown did not begin with the six-day Creation.

The 7000-year countdown was tragically initiated by the sin of Adam and has been amplified and magnified by his descendants in an ever increasing crescendo of unspeakable tragedy.

The 7000-year countdown starting the moment Adam sinned has been characterized by a cycle of dispensations that all end exactly the same way.

No matter what new experiment is attempted to govern the wicked heart of man it always ends the same.

Whether it is anarchy or tyranny, democracy or socialism, whether ruled by many laws or few, whether governed by judges, kings, or God Himself, it always ends the same way.

Man's heart betrays all forms of governance, it rebels against everything that is good and holy as it reveals itself to be wicked, untamable and rebellious and self-destructive.

There is only one solution to this problem and it is not within the power of man to exercise its promise or potency. Man is in desperate need of a new heart, a recreated nature that is joyfully in glorious harmony with his creator.

Is this the lesson that man is to learn as he arrogantly schemes and plans his utopian fantasies? Man, without God, cannot achieve the latest version of an upgraded and improved Man. It is madness to think that aided by superintelligence and technology, the false promise that echoes from the serpent's malicious lies, will accomplish what only God the creator can accomplish.

And what is that?

A NEW HEART!

The first word in the Bible, Berisheet, reveals a millennial perspective that is so accurate and precise at forecasting the past, that we dare not ignore what it forecast for the future.

It is no wonder God has NOT disclosed this before now, saving it for the final generation. The generation living in the last fleeting years of time. Time that is passing quickly and moving with speed toward the next event that God has ordained to happen both "Just in Time" and at the exact appointed time on His millennial day for a 1000-year calendar.

To be precise, you are literally living on the razor's edge of a nearly 2000-year countdown that is only a few short years from completion.

You are living in a "time of signs" that have not been seen since the time of Noah.

The corruption of man has reached the boiling point, the inflection point when iniquity overflows the cup of God's patience and mercy.

You're living in the generation that has seen the fulfillment of the one event that notifies all the earth that God is Sovereign over all the affairs of men and nations. We have been a witness to the most unlikely historical event to ever take place in human history.

Sunset with the flag of Israel waving over Jerusalem

The miracle of the regathering and re-establishment of the Nation of Israel is no longer a pipe dream believed by a fringe group of biblical literalists. Nor is it explained away by the faithless Bible teachers who are so brilliant at allegorizing and spiritualizing away God's promises and filling those that follow them with an arrogance and pride that is astonishing in the face of God's literal fulfillment of His unbreakable promises.

Israel has been brought back to their land in unbelief just as the Lord both promised and foretold.

This generation has witnessed the coming together with intensity and frequency the earth signs of earthquakes, pestilence, wars, famine, tornado, hurricane, tsunamis and volcanic eruption that Jesus said would accelerate in a chorus of converging ever increasing cycles of calamitous prominence that He compared to birth pains. Birth pains that have never before been witnessed by any previous generation.

Even the most hardened sinner living outside of the influence of God's Spirit knows that something is wrong and something frightful is on the near horizon.

The children of light, according to the Apostle Paul, will not be overtaken by the DAY. The day that the Prince of Heaven slips through the open window of time that has been allocated from the beginning to demonstrate God's grace to the nations, the time we call the Church Age. The Children of Light know the season of the Lord's return is upon us.

This generation has witnessed numerous signs.

There are signs in the Heavens, signs in the earth, signs in the unseen world of evil spirits manifesting in our time and space dimension, signs all around us that are prophesied to cause fear in the hardened hearts of those who have rejected God's Anointed One.

Signs that are meant to encourage and increase to the point of exuberance the blessed hope that is the birthright of every Christian pilgrim in the world. Pilgrims who long with all their heart to be escorted in the twinkling of an eye into the presence of our Lord and Savior. Taken to the place Jesus said He was going to prepare for us in Heaven.

Christians who were once only occasionally vexed by the downward tip-toeing into the dark shadowy corners of sin are now shocked by the plunge into the septic dank sewer of depravity and disorder that is happening on a wholesale basis all around us.

For these discouraged Saints, the Lord is unsealing a revelation hidden from all the other generations that lived on the earth, preserved for the unveiling to the final terminal generation in order that Christians would be courageous in the last moments of time. Christians must ensure these moments are not wasted on sleep but rather moments in which we are meant to AWAKEN and LOOK UP with eyes filled with faith and hope in spite of all the forces of evil that war against the simple truth that our Salvation draweth nigh, and is even now at the door.

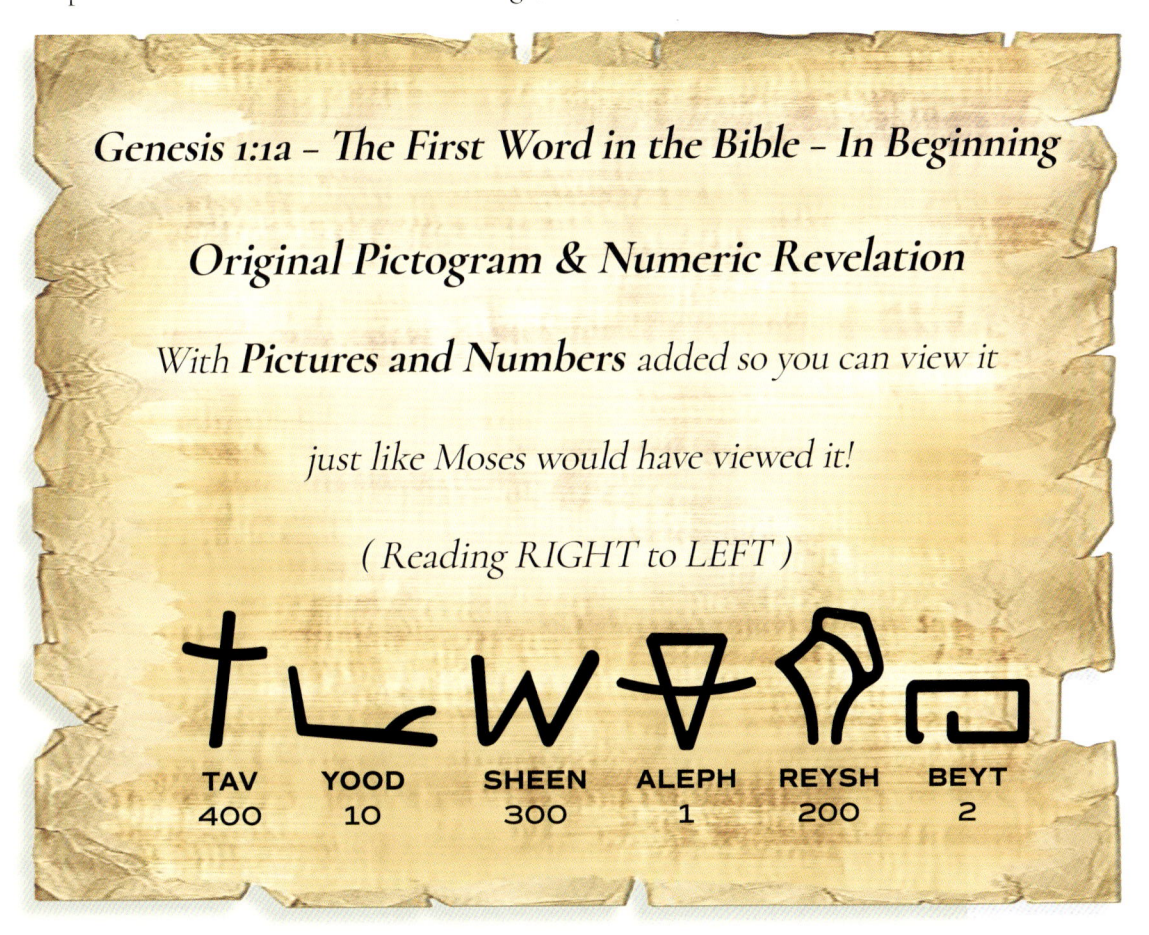

Genesis 1:1a – The First Word in the Bible – In Beginning

Original Pictogram & Numeric Revelation

With **Pictures and Numbers** added so you can view it

just like Moses would have viewed it!

(Reading RIGHT to LEFT)

TAV	YOOD	SHEEN	ALEPH	REYSH	BEYT
400	10	300	1	200	2

We are now ready to disclose the two remaining and final time-stamp revelations found in the very first word in the Bible exactly where we began this inquiry. Let's read the words of the LORD as recorded by Isaiah the prophet one more time.

> ## Isaiah 46:9-10a
> *Remember the former things of old:*
> *for I am God, and there is none else;*
> *I am God, and there is none like me,*
> *Declaring the end from the beginning,*

There are two more TIME-STAMP revelations in the Berisheet Prophecy that will literally fulfill the declaration made by God as recorded by Isaiah the prophet. Declaring the End from the Beginning.

The Berisheet FIRE Prophecy

In the first part of the Berisheet prophecy we discovered that the first word in the Bible, the Hebrew word Berisheet, the word literally translated IN BEGINNING, was not just about one beginning but contained a prophetic picture and number revelation that heralded multiple beginnings, with one major thematic beginning in view that overshadowed all the others.

You might have guessed that the Berisheet Prophecy was about the six-day Creation miracle followed by the seventh day of rest, but it was not.

Instead, we discovered the beginning that heralded the 7000-years of sin and rebellion that began with the sin of Adam 33-33.5 years after Creation. And what beginning was it that forecast the year Adam sinned?

It was the beginning that took place in the 4th millennium on God's calendar, the beginning that took place on Mount Moriah where the greatest accomplishment to ever take place in human history was manifested on a wooden cross that lifted up the Prince of Heaven who had humbled Himself and come to earth as Immanuel, God incarnate, in order to satisfy the sin debt of Adam and all his children, including you and me.

Now we will unfold the two remaining millennial time-stamp prophecies that are just waiting to be revealed.

Let's see if we can discover the prophetic timeline and the picture prophecy that literally fulfills the Isaiah 46 prophecy.

Let's see if we can find the End from the Beginning in the first word God revealed to man...the word Berisheet that literally means "In Beginning."

It is unusual, to say the least, to find even one word nested inside another word in the Hebrew language. But to find 5 Hebrew words nested in one Hebrew word is clearly astounding and obviously meant to arrest our attention.

We have already identified four of those Hebrew words that we found nested in the six letter Hebrew word Berisheet.

Can you remember what they were?

Let's review them:

Beyt - IN or INSIDE

Beyt Reysh pronounced Bar is the Hebrew word for - **SON**

Beyt Reysh Aleph pronounced Bara is the Hebrew word - **CREATED**

Reysh Aleph Sheen pronounced Reysh is the Hebrew word for the - **HEAD PERSON - PRINCE - the FIRST**

These four words were obviously nested in the revelation in order that it might clearly notify us that the:

- Son of God was in the House.
- The Son of God came out of His House.

It also disclosed to our amazement why the Son of God came out of His Heavenly Home.

Amazingly there is one more important word nested in Berisheet.

The Son of God came Out of His House.

THE BERISHEET END-TIMES PASSOVER PROPHECY | 61
CHAPTER 3: THE BERISHEET END-TIMES PASSOVER PROPHECY

The Hebrew word spelled **Aleph Sheen**.

Aleph is the third and **Sheen** is the fourth letter in Berisheet.

The picture meaning of **Aleph Sheen** is pretty easy to figure out based on the pictures.

Aleph, pictured as an OX, represents strength.

Sheen pictured as TEETH is meant to convey the idea of crushing and destroying, like the gnashing of teeth.

Put the **Aleph** and the **Sheen** together and you have the picture of **STRONG DESTRUCTION**.

Do we know what strong destruction God has in mind?

We have already seen how **Sheen** was used as a picture to forecast the cross.

Is there another crushing and destroying on the horizon?

The answer is yes and God leaves us in no doubt as to what will cause the destruction.

Aleph Sheen, the fifth Hebrew word nested in Berisheet, literally means **FIRE!**

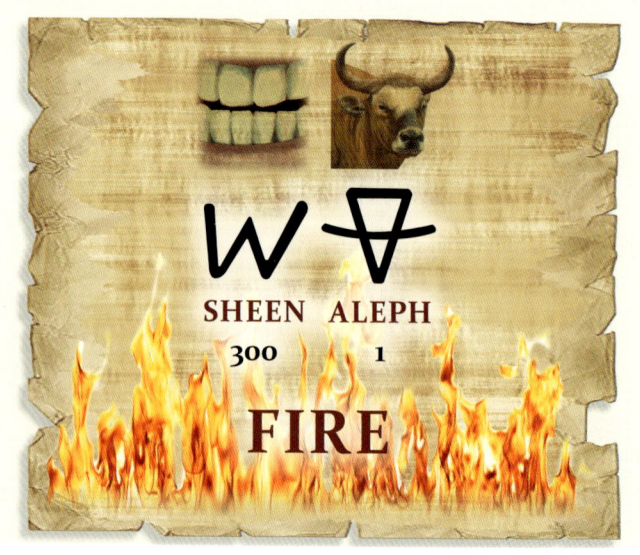

The Yood and the Sheen tell us when this FIRE is scheduled to take place on God's millennial calendar.

When is this going to take place?

YOOD 10   X   SHEEN 300 = 3000 years

3000 years from the center point of man's history, the date of the Cross in 30 AD, the Berisheet Prophecy is forecasting FIRE.

Anyone who has read the Bible does not need to guess as to what this single, shocking word is forecasting.

Our present world is going to END in a fiery conflagration!

When is this going to happen?

We now know the answer based on the Berisheet End-Times Passover Prophecy.

Starting from the center point of all history in 30 AD and then adding 3000 years takes us just over 1000-years into the future to the year 3030 AD.

Based on our discussion of the timeline, 3030 AD would be exactly 7000-years from the year Adam sinned and was expelled from the Garden of Eden 33-33.5 years after Creation.

The Berisheet Prophecy makes it pretty unambiguous, 3030 AD marks the end of the 7000-year countdown allotted to man.

And what is it that comes to an end after 7000 years? 7000 years marks the complete destruction of our present Heaven and Earth.

The answer is what puts this back into God's Millennial Perspective.

Seven is one of four sacred numbers that means **DIVINE COMPLETION**, and you do not need to have a PHD in Theology to figure out what **COMES TO AN END** after 7000 years.

Sin, rebellion and everything it touched and corrupted, including the very world that God pronounced good in the very beginning, has become polluted. These things, along with sin and rebellion, must come to an end.

Fire not only marks the end of the 7th millennium it also inaugurates the beginning of a new sinless eternity heralded by the creation of a new Heaven and a new Earth.

It is the appointed time when God will roll up the current Heavens and Earth like a scroll and put a match to it, just as declared in His word.

Listen to what it says in the New Testament book of 2nd Peter.

2 Peter 3:7

But the Heavens and the earth, which are now, by the same word are kept in store, reserved unto fire against the day of judgment and perdition of ungodly men.

2 Peter 3:12

Looking for and hasting unto the coming of the day of God, wherein the Heavens being on fire shall be dissolved, and the elements shall melt with fervent heat.

God said He would declare the End from the Beginning and He has done it literally with a precision that cannot be denied.

The Prophecy in Isaiah has literally been fulfilled in the Beginning, literally in the revelation of His WORD Beginning. God has declared the End from the Beginning.

And He did it in a way no one could have ever dreamed.

God accomplished His Word from the center point of history in 30 AD. It is from that Divinely appointed time that we can date the six days of creation followed by the 7th day of rest.

The Creation event took place in the year 4004 BC. This was followed by 33-33.5 years of innocence in the Garden of Eden that ended abruptly with the sin of Adam 33-33.5 years from the start date for Creation. And now we know that the end of the present Heaven and earth is scheduled to perish by fire in the year 3030 AD.

We are now living roughly a thousand-years before the final fulfillment the 7th day Sabbath Millennial Perspective that will end 7000 years of sin and rebellion.

We are now left with one more time-stamp prophecy—the final Berisheet Prophecy.

Like the other two before it, the Lord has left little doubt about what this prophecy is about.

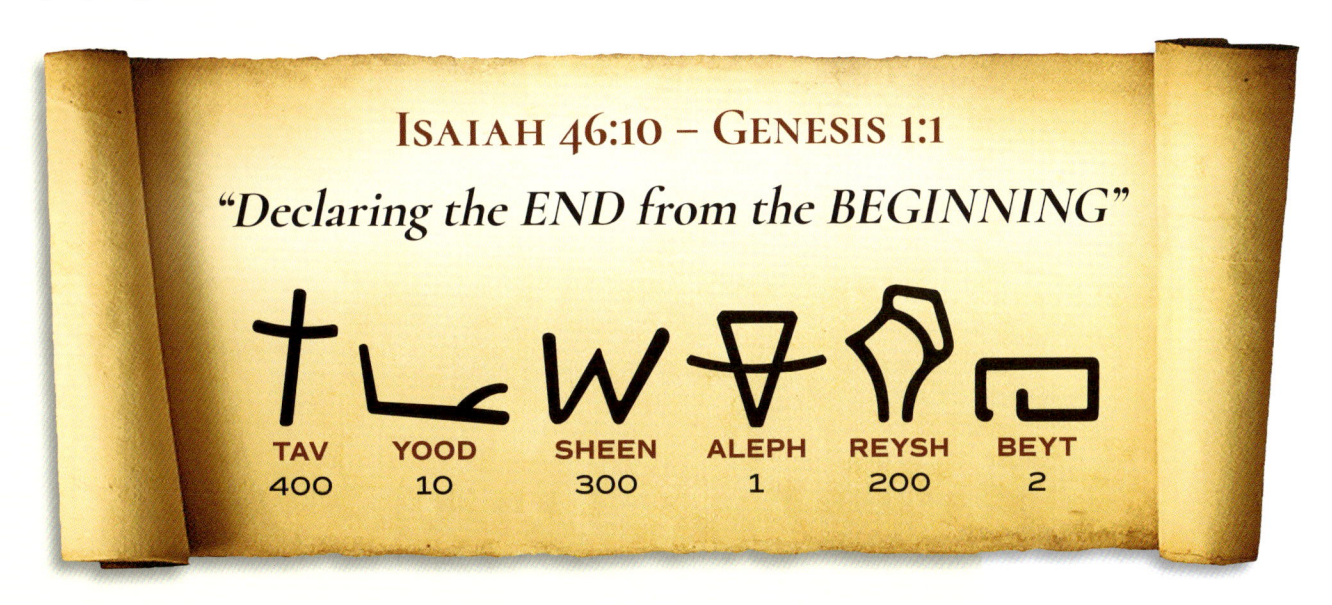

ISAIAH 46:10 – GENESIS 1:1

"Declaring the END from the BEGINNING"

TAV	YOOD	SHEEN	ALEPH	REYSH	BEYT
400	10	300	1	200	2

Sabbath Millennial End-Times Perspective Reset by Berisheet Revelation!

God's Final Countdown for Fallen Man Begins with the Cross, Not Creation.

10 Yood X 400 † Yood Tav = The Cross – 4000 - 30 AD † CENTER POINT

Creation 4004 BC   Sin of Adam 3970 AD   Crucifixion of Christ - 30 AD

10 Yood X 300 W Yood Sheen – New Heaven & Earth – 3000 + 30 AD †

Destruction of Present Heaven & Earth and Creation of
NEW Heaven & Earth 3030 AD (7000 years from the Sin of Adam)

10 Yood X 200 Reysh Yood Reysh – The Second Coming – 2000 + 30 AD †

Yood the number 10 signals that a plan has been ordained in Heaven.

A prophecy that will unfold when the Reysh, the Prince of glory, leaves His home one more time in order to accomplish the next phase of the unfolding plan that His Father in Heaven purposed before the foundation of the world.

But this time the Reysh, the Prince of Glory, will not be coming as the Sacrificial Lamb to be mocked, beaten and killed.

No, The Son of God will be coming out of His home in Heaven with a ROAR and the shout of victory. He will be coming as the conquering Lion of Judah.

King Jesus is soon coming to establish His 1000-year kingdom on the earth.

The King is now waiting in Heaven for exactly the right moment at the appointed time to come again as the conquering King of the whole earth.

When is this going to happen?

TAV	YOOD	SHEEN	ALEPH	REYSH	BEYT
400	10	300	1	200	2

The answer is found in the picture of the Reysh the PRINCE coming out of His home to accomplish the Yood, the PLAN. The pictures that reveal this event also reveals when this event is going to happen on God's millennial calendar.

The time-stamp of 2000 years or two millennia added to the 30 AD Berisheet End-Times Passover Prophecy gives us the answer.

Startling as it may seem, the year of Christ's Second coming is no longer thousands of years into the future as it was in the first-century church. It is upon us, it is forecast to happen based on the Berisheet End-Times Passover Prophecy in the year 2030 AD.

10 X 200 = 2000

The Berisheet End-Times Passover Prophecy forecast that two thousand-years from the crucifixion date of 30 AD the Lord is coming to establish His Kingdom here on the earth.

The Berisheet Prophecy
Isaiah 46:10 – Genesis 1:1
"Declaring the END from the BEGINNING"

TAV	YOOD	SHEEN	ALEPH	REYSH	BEYT
400	10	300	1	200	2

Sabbath Millennial End-Times Perspective Clarified by Berisheet Revelation!

God's Final Countdown for Fallen Man Begins with the Cross Not Creation.

10 x 400 Yood Tav – The **Cross** Time-Stamp **4000 years**

10 x 300 Yood Sheen – The **End of the Age** Time-Stamp – **3000 years**

10 x 200 Yood Reysh – The **Second Coming** Time-Stamp – **2000 years**

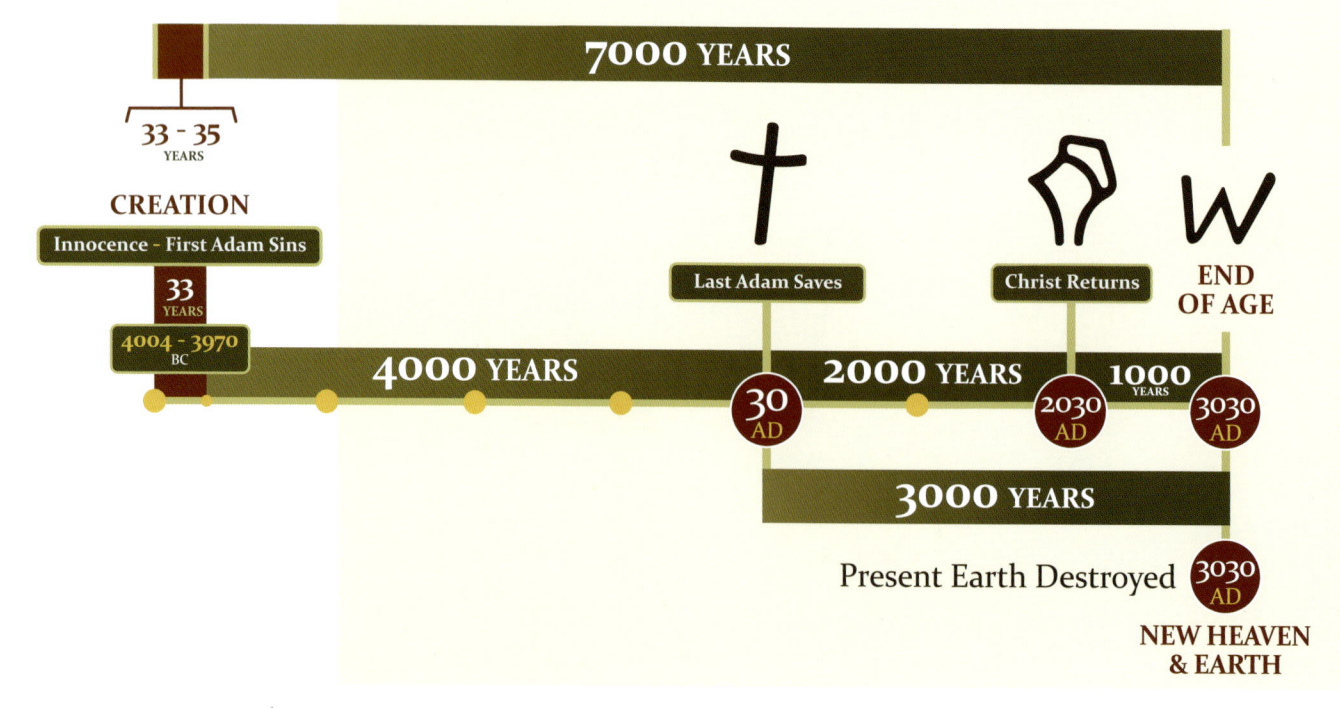

7000 YEARS

33 - 35 YEARS

CREATION
Innocence – First Adam Sins
33 YEARS
4004 – 3970 BC

4000 YEARS — Last Adam Saves — 30 AD — **2000 YEARS** — Christ Returns — 2030 AD — **1000 YEARS** — END OF AGE — 3030 AD

3000 YEARS

Present Earth Destroyed — 3030 AD

NEW HEAVEN & EARTH

---

68 | THE BERISHEET END-TIMES PASSOVER PROPHECY
C.J. LOVIK

This is where people, including many Christians, are all mixed up and confused. The coming of the Lord that NO one knows the day or the hour of is not the Second Coming of Christ, but the Coming of Christ to collect His church.

If you are confused about this, I would suggest you open your Bible and start making a list of all the verses that describe the coming of Christ in the New Testament. What you will discover is that there are least 20 categories that either highlight major contradictions in the Bible or 20 categories that describe two different events.

The Departure of the Church, popularly called the Rapture, is not the same as the Second Coming of Christ.

The Coming of Christ in the clouds to collect His church has as its purpose the escorting of Saints off the earth, the earth that is about to experience the wrath of God.

The Second Coming is all about Christ coming with His saints to establish a 1000-year kingdom here on the earth.

The Second Coming event has so many prophetic time-stamps and signs connected to its arrival that it is hard to keep track of them all. Obviously, anyone who has a Bible during the great tribulation can consult it and know exactly when the Second Coming is going to occur. Anyone that tells you that no one now knows or ever will know the year that Christ is coming again is either ignorant of the facts or confused.

The Coming of Christ in the clouds.

To be clear, the Berisheet Prophecy does not forecast the year when Christ is going to come and collect His Church, but it does forecast the season.

The translation of the pictures and numbers in the first word in the Bible reveals three time-stamped events that are all based on a fourth event, the one event God has magnified above all others, the center point of all history, the Cross event that took place in 30 AD.

Just HOW MANY BEGINNINGS are forecast in the Berisheet End-Times Passover Prophecy? If we count the Cross are there four events directly forecast in the first Prophecy in the Bible?

Based on the Millennial Day for a thousand-years perspective, we can now put a time-line on a couple other important events that are now for the first time clearly in view and time-stamped based on the Berisheet Prophecy.

Amazingly, the Berisheet Prophecy reveals SEVEN Beginnings, all knowable and arranged in order on God's Millennial Calendar.

Let's briefly review all 7 prophetic Beginnings.

1. 4004 BC – The Six-Day Miracle Creation Beginning followed by the 7th day of Rest.

2. 3970 BC – The Beginning of Sin and Rebellion - The Year Adam Sinned, 33-33.5 years after Creation.

3. 30 AD – The New Beginning that Opened up the Way to Heaven based on the atoning death of the Last Adam, Jesus the Christ who accomplished our salvation on a wooden cross as prophesied in 30 AD. The Beginning of the Church Age.

4. The Departure of the Church. The New Beginning highlighted for believers by a new

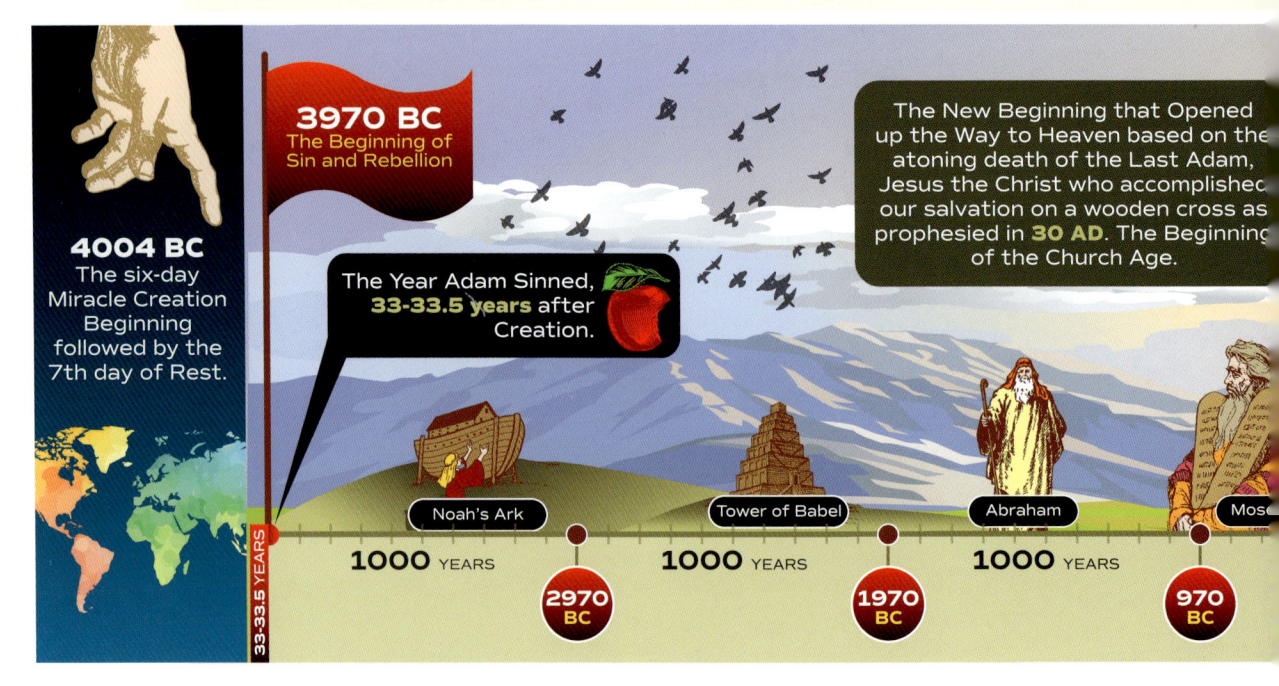

glorified body fit and made for Heaven and perfected in order that we might enjoy our Lord and Savior as we are blest beyond reason to be in His presence forever.

5 2023 AD – Daniel's 70th Week, also known as the Great Tribulation that lasts seven years and precedes with no time gap, the Second Coming of Christ.

The Beginning of Sorrows for the World and the Beginning of Discipline for God's beloved Children of Israel who will go under the rod of discipline in order that they might finally call upon with eyes that have been opened by faith to finally receive Yeshua Ha-Mashiach.

6 2030 – The Second Coming of Christ. The Beginning of the Millennial Reign of Christ on the earth for 1000-years.

7 3030 – The End of the Present Heaven and Earth and the Creation of a new eternal Heaven and Earth. The Beginning of the Eternal State.

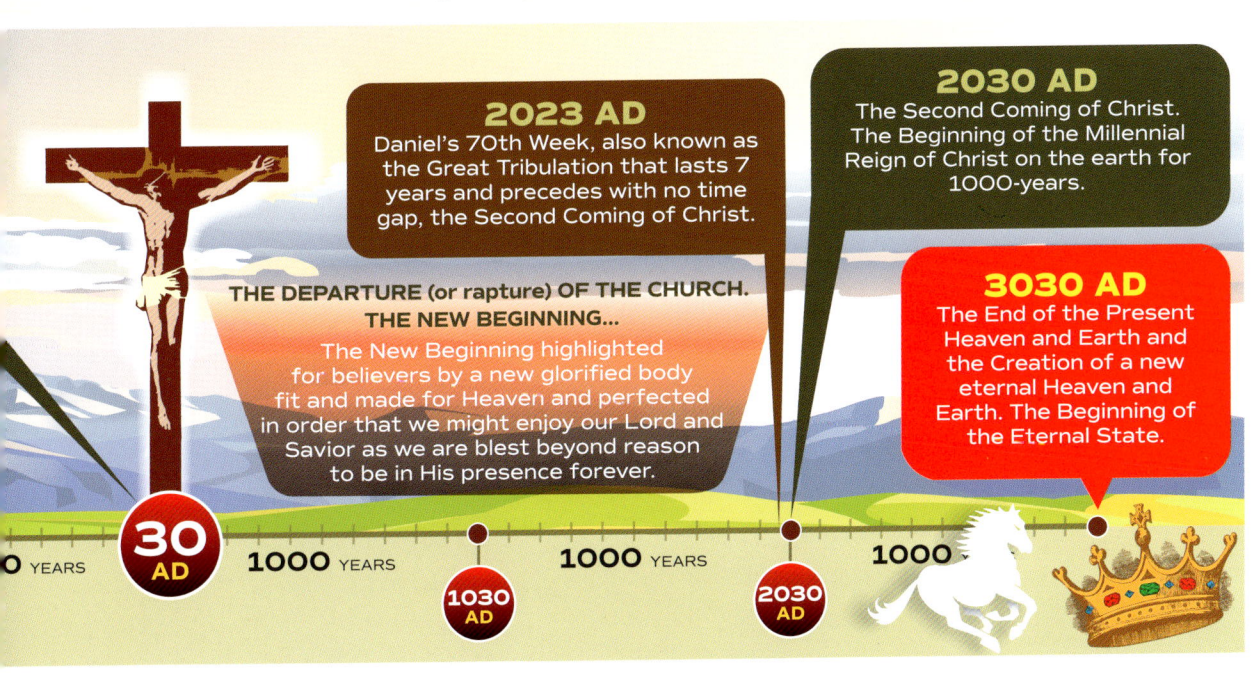

2023 AD
Daniel's 70th Week, also known as the Great Tribulation that lasts 7 years and precedes with no time gap, the Second Coming of Christ.

2030 AD
The Second Coming of Christ. The Beginning of the Millennial Reign of Christ on the earth for 1000-years.

THE DEPARTURE (or rapture) OF THE CHURCH. THE NEW BEGINNING...
The New Beginning highlighted for believers by a new glorified body fit and made for Heaven and perfected in order that we might enjoy our Lord and Savior as we are blest beyond reason to be in His presence forever.

3030 AD
The End of the Present Heaven and Earth and the Creation of a new eternal Heaven and Earth. The Beginning of the Eternal State.

0 YEARS | 30 AD | 1000 YEARS | 1030 AD | 1000 YEARS | 2030 AD | 1000

THE BERISHEET END-TIMES PASSOVER PROPHECY
CHAPTER 3: THE BERISHEET END-TIMES PASSOVER PROPHECY

You will notice that I did not forecast a year for the Departure of the Church.

We do not know the date of the Departure of the Church.

No, but we know the season just like the Lord said we would.

Let me explain.

There is currently an OPEN window of time through which the Lord is going to slip through and collect His church.

That window of time has been slowly closing for almost 2000 years and is now almost shut.

We know that the departure of the Church could happen at any time, and now we know that while it could quickly close today, it will slam shut no later than 2023, the same year that begins the seven-year Great Tribulation also known as Daniel's 70th week.

We would wish to know the precise date of the Departure of the Church

The window of time that was fully open nearly 2000 years wide in 30 AD is now only open five years wide as of the production of this book in March of 2018.

Does that mean we have 5 years before Christ comes to gather us into His presence and take us home based on our proposed 30 AD cross event?

No, it means that we could have up to 6 years before Christ comes to gather us into His presence. Or we could have only minutes before we are in His presence in the blink of an eye.

The Berisheet End-Times Passover Prophecy is a set of very simple, forthright, and easy to understand puzzle pieces made up of pictures and numbers. Once assembled, the Berisheet End-Times Passover Prophecy contains the forecast that the Church of Christ will not exist on the earth after the year 2023, based on the cross event date of 30 AD.

It may not exist on the earth after 2022, or 2021 or tomorrow, only God knows.

Remember that the Church was a mystery not revealed in the Old Testament. Is it a surprise that the exact day and hour that the Bride Groom is coming to collect His Bride, His Church, is also a mystery?

But while we do not know the exact day or time of day we can forecast the number of years left in the open space of the window of God's Grace through which the Son of God will come in the clouds to collect His glorified church body.

Let me ask the Christians reading this amazing end-time perspective a question. *Are you anxiously awaiting your Lord's return?* If you are then this revelation should be greatly encouraging to you. There is just a little more time, be patient and keep living your life as if He was going to return today; He may.

Or, are you a confessing Christian immersed in the cares of this world, in love with its tantalizing distractions, pleasures and attractions that like a siren song cry out for your attention? Does the thought of the Lord's coming soon sound like an inconvenient truth you truly hope is not to be taken seriously?

If the news that the coming of the Lord is going to really happen and soon does not elevate your spirit to heights of glorious anticipation then something is wrong with your life of faith and you need to repent of it and get your eyes back on Jesus alone before you are standing before Him consumed by shame and regret.

The Berisheet Prophecy is the most amazing warning you will ever hear in this lifetime. Heed it and get back to loving the Lord who redeemed you with His precious blood and return Him to the center of your life where He belongs.

The Son of God will come in the clouds to collect church

THE BERISHEET END-TIMES PASSOVER PROPHECY
CHAPTER 3: THE BERISHEET END-TIMES PASSOVER PROPHECY

If you're not a Christian, I would plead with you not to perish. Come to Christ while there is still time. Before the one thing you have taken for granted slips away and is lost forever - time.

You may think you have all the time in the world.

The Berisheet Passover Prophecy has been revealed to you so that you might know that the appointed time for the Church of Jesus Christ to be joined with their Savior is only moments away. You do not want to be left on the earth after that event takes place.

If you are not a Christian, it is time for you to acknowledge your sin and your desperate need for a Savior. It is time to pray for God's mercy and grace as you look with eyes of faith to the One who shed His precious blood so that you might be redeemed and claim the promise that has been written for your encouragement and redemption.

Consider this message with the understanding that it was sent to you in order that you might escape the wrath to come.

Romans 10:9-10

That if thou shalt confess with thy mouth the Lord Jesus, and shalt believe in thine heart that God hath raised him from the dead, thou shalt be saved.

For with the heart man believeth unto righteousness; and with the mouth confession is made unto salvation.

This concludes the general outline of the translation of the first prophecy revealed in the Bible.

Revealed but hidden in the Beginning so that you might be warned at the appointed time that Christ is coming to collect His Church.

The Berisheet Prophecy is all about Beginnings and Endings from a Divine perspective. In this outlook, the big events on the calendar are spanned by exactly 1000-year exact periods of time that from God's vantage point are days.

Just like God put an exact boundary around one day, it being twenty-four hours divided into a period called day and a period called night, both those periods when combined equaling 24 hours.

Jesus confirmed this in John 11:9 when He asked, "Are there not 12 hours in a day?"

The rest of this book is devoted to filling in the blanks and answering the questions raised in the first 5 chapters.

We begin with an overview of God's day for a thousand-year outlook.

Just what exactly is the Sabbath Millennial Prophetic Perspective and why should I care?

This will be followed by an examination of the eight time-spans that we can now correctly "date" based on the single event that God has established as a center point from which all other time prophecies can be forecast from this one Event.

The Sabbath Millennial Prophetic Perspective is ancient.

The new start-date based on the revelation of the Berisheet End-Times Passover Prophecy is not. Neither is it new or novel, it was simply a prophecy hidden from the very beginning in the beginning. I believe this simple, easy to understand and biblically harmonious re-set date has been reserved for disclosure at exactly the appointed time.

I believe that time has come. I believe the second hand on God's prophetic clock is ready to tick off the final seconds that will result in the end of one thing and the beginning of something new.

I believe the events forecast in the Berisheet Prophecy, the first prophecy in the Bible, are going to happen in quick succession, revealing monumental prophetic events.

I believe that the next three events on God's calendar are all going to happen in the next twelve years, starting from the publication date of this book in 2018.

It is the purpose of this book to reveal to Christians the events that we can expect to transpire, in order. The purpose of this book is to encourage Christians to be mindful that they are living in the last moments of time, to rethink their cozy relationship with the world and those that dwell on it, and to make themselves ready to meet the Lord.

This book is a last end-times warning for Christians to wake up and look up with faith and overflowing hearts filled with hope.

Luke 21:28
And when these things begin to come to pass, then look up, and lift up your heads; for your redemption draweth nigh.

We will begin by answering the following question:

What is Sabbath Millennial Prophetic Perspective and why does it matter?

CHAPTER 4

Sabbath-Millennial Prophetic Perspective

> According to Exodus, the Sabbath is a day of rest on the seventh day, commanded by God to be kept as a holy day of rest, as God rested from creation.

Why should you care about the Sabbath-Millennial Prophetic Perspective?

The answer is simple and profound.

The answer is because men of God in the past, including ancient Jewish Sages and Rabbis along with most of the early church fathers, believed in the Sabbath-Millennial Prophetic Perspective.

Sabbath-Millennial Prophetic Perspective is the only enduring ancient prophetic outlook that is based on the literal interpretation of the Bible.

The early apostles, taught by Jesus, had this perspective. Jesus never disabused them of this outlook.

Let's listen to what Barnabas the Apostle who was the missionary partner of the Apostle Paul as mentioned in the book of Acts 14:4, taught the converts to Jesus Christ as recorded in his Epistle, published sometime before 61 AD.

For many the Epistle of Barnabas was considered to be equal to Scripture. Obviously, the Epistle of Barnabas was not included in the Canon of Scripture, but it is historical and should be considered as such.

Some of the early church fathers, including Tertullian, identify Barnabas as the author of the book of Hebrews. This attribution points out how highly esteemed Barnabas was by both the apostles and the early church fathers.

Did Barnabas actually write the book of Hebrews?

While it is very possible, no one really knows for sure.

Paul and Barnabas undertook the first missionary journeys into the Gentile regions where they preached the Gospel and defended those gentiles that believed against the Judaizers of the day.

The Epistle of Barnabas presents the Creation Week as a pattern for human history with one day equaling one thousand years. Barnabas believed that there would be six thousand years of human history followed by a Sabbath rest on the seventh day.

The Sabbath-Millennial Prophetic Perspective is outlined in the Epistle of Barnabas 15:3-5, translated from Greek to English by JB Lightfoot.

Hear what the Apostle Barnabas has to say about the Sabbath-Millennial Prophetic Perspective in his own words.

Read What Barnabas the Missionary partner of the Apostle Paul has to say about the Sabbath-Millennial Prophetic Perspective

Barnabas 15:3-5

Of the Sabbath He speaketh in the beginning of the Creation; And God made the works of His hands in six days, and He ended on the seventh day, and rested on it, and He hallowed it. Give heed, children, what this meaneth; He ended in six days.

He meaneth this, that in six thousand years the Lord shall bring all things to an end; for the day with Him signifyeth a thousand years; and this He himself beareth me witness, saying; Behold, the day of the Lord shall be as a thousand years. Therefore, children, in six days, that is in six thousand years, everything shall come to an end.

And He rested on the seventh day, this He meaneth; when His Son shall come, and shall abolish the time of the Lawless One, and shall judge the ungodly, and shall change the sun and the moon and the stars, then shall he truly rest on the seventh day.

Where did Barnabas and others get this day for a 1000-year perspective?

The Day Adam Died!

Let's examine some of the clues starting with The Day Adam Died.

Adam was told that if he ignored God's instruction and ate of the Tree of the Knowledge of Good and Evil, that **in that day** he would die.

Adam disobeyed and died 930 years later.

What are we missing?

Day for a Thousand-Year clue

Did God change His mind and decide to add 327,620 days to the life of Adam? (Is there a clue in the math?)

Is the Bible to be taken literally or are we to expect rounding errors that are off by a factor of 327,620?

We know that Adam's life spanned a period of 930 years before he physically died.

We know that God told Adam that the day he ate the forbidden fruit he would die.

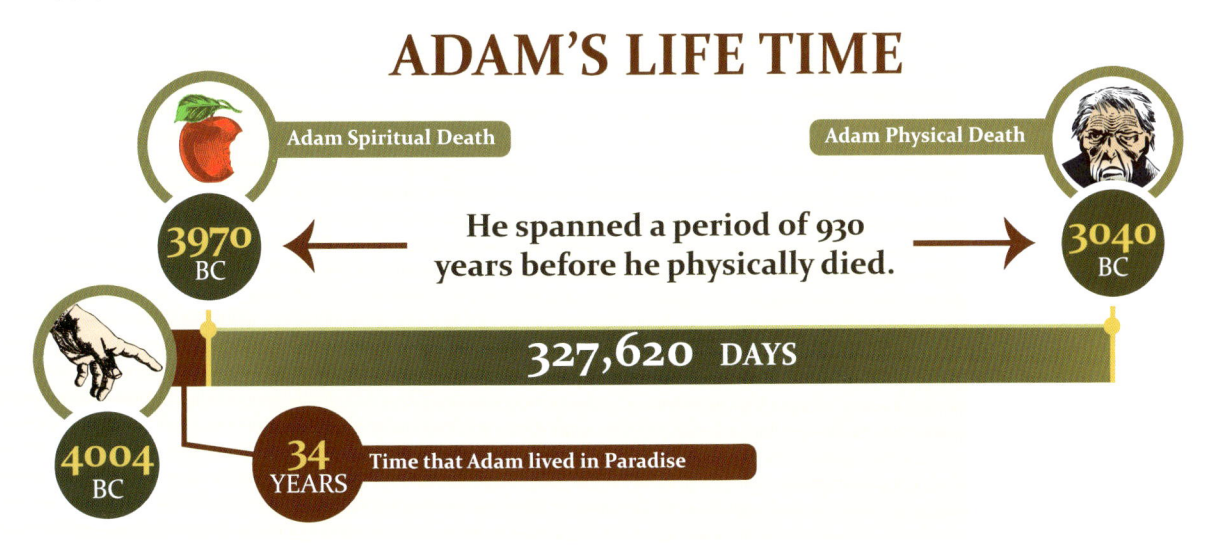

ADAM'S LIFE TIME

Adam Spiritual Death — 3970 BC
Adam Physical Death — 3040 BC
He spanned a period of 930 years before he physically died.
4004 BC
327,620 DAYS
34 YEARS — Time that Adam lived in Paradise

Did Adam die the day he disobeyed and rebelled against his Heavenly Father?

Obviously, there is a misunderstanding of monumental proportions when it comes to how man measures time, or is something else going on?

Could it be that this mystery of time is a secret purposely hidden in the numbers of the Creation story in order that we might gain wisdom and insight as we consider the days of history and the days of our lives?

Perhaps it is a puzzle that has been revealed in order that our way of thinking and calculating time comes in line with God's method of timing the events He has planned for mankind.

If this is true, then the mystery is not there simply to be solved in order to satisfy our curiosity.

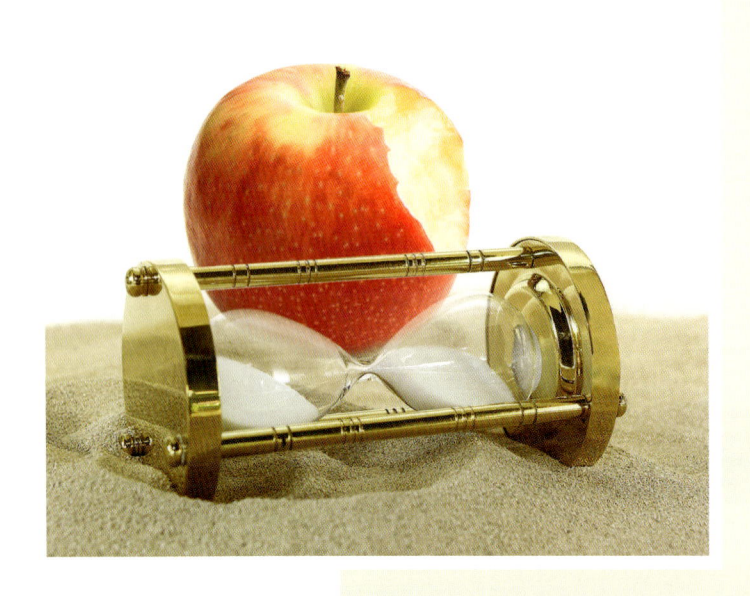

Apparently, the mystery is meant to stir up questions that once answered will give us wisdom and understanding. Wisdom that does not come from the forbidden tree, but from the mind of God. Wisdom that lifts us out of the confusion and chaos. Raising us above the moment by moment hum-drum of ticking time that all seems to connect to the past and the future in ways that appear to have no fruitful purpose.

The key to understanding God's puzzling use of the word "day" in relation to the death of Adam is mentioned in the both the Old and New Testament Scripture.

The ONE THING Saint Peter wants us to know!

Read what Peter the disciple of Yeshua discloses about the Lord's command of time:

> ## 2 Peter 3:8
> *But, beloved, be not ignorant of this one thing, that one day is with the Lord as a thousand-years, and a thousand-years as one day.*

Could this be the puzzle piece that is missing?

Are we meant to consider two deaths, one spiritual and the other physical both happening in one day?

The physical death of Adam lingered over a period that is hard for us to imagine based on our own experience that is tethered to a 70-80 year time-span.

Maybe that is the point.

Adam and Eve both died spiritually the day they sinned. This obvious conclusion seems to satisfy the curious and is usually all the attention this time-riddle is given.

Has anyone ever thought to consider the obvious point the Lord was making about both spiritual and physical death?

The physical Adam shriveled up and died over a period of time just shy of 1000-years. Adam's life and death can be compared to a ripened apple stripped from the tree from which it receives its nourishment and life.

The Adam that survived the day of disobedience withered and shriveled away slowly over centuries of time coming just 70 years shy of 1000-years.

Is this a clue?

Was it the essence of Adam that was attached to God, like grapes are attached to the grapevine? Once severed from the vine they shrivel up separated from the source of life.

Is that a picture of the death of Adam, an instant death that results in a slow return to the dust from which he was created?

Is that the "detachment" that God calls death?

We all glibly solve the riddle and move on with the one answer that seems to satisfy our curiosity but never fully grasps the rough edges of the truth that is staring us in the face.

If we are to take God's Word literally then we must ask, what is a day?

Is it a 24-hour cycling period divided into light and the absence of light?

The answer is yes!

Does God expect us to be able to entertain two concepts at the same time, drawing conclusions from both that prepare us for the revelation of God's plans for mankind over TIME?

It is certainly worth thinking about.

Adam spiritually died the very moment, and in the day that he sinned.

The physical Adam retains his life for 930 years, almost 340,000 days.

That is a long time by men's reckoning. We are hopeful to reach three score and ten years, just over 25,000 days.

Why did God allow Adam this generous amount of time to live out his physical life on earth?

God created 24-hour days on a physical earth designed as man's home.

God could have easily taken Adam's physical life the same day his spiritual life was extinguished.

"Death of Adam." Piero della Francesca. 1466.

But He didn't for a reason. Could the reason be connected with the revelation that man did not have all the time in the world but was limited to 7000 years?

Are the Six Literal Days of Creation a Prophetic Harbinger of the Sabbath-Millennial Perspective?

God reveals that He reckons days relative to His plans for man in terms of millenniums.

This is the key to understanding the six days of Creation concluding with a seventh day of rest.

To be very clear, I am not suggesting that each day of Creation was actually 1000-years.

That is clearly not what God disclosed in the book of Genesis.

Each day was one twenty-four hour period of time consisting of equal periods of daylight and the absence of it.

Each twenty-four day and night cycle are repeated for 7 days and then it begins again.

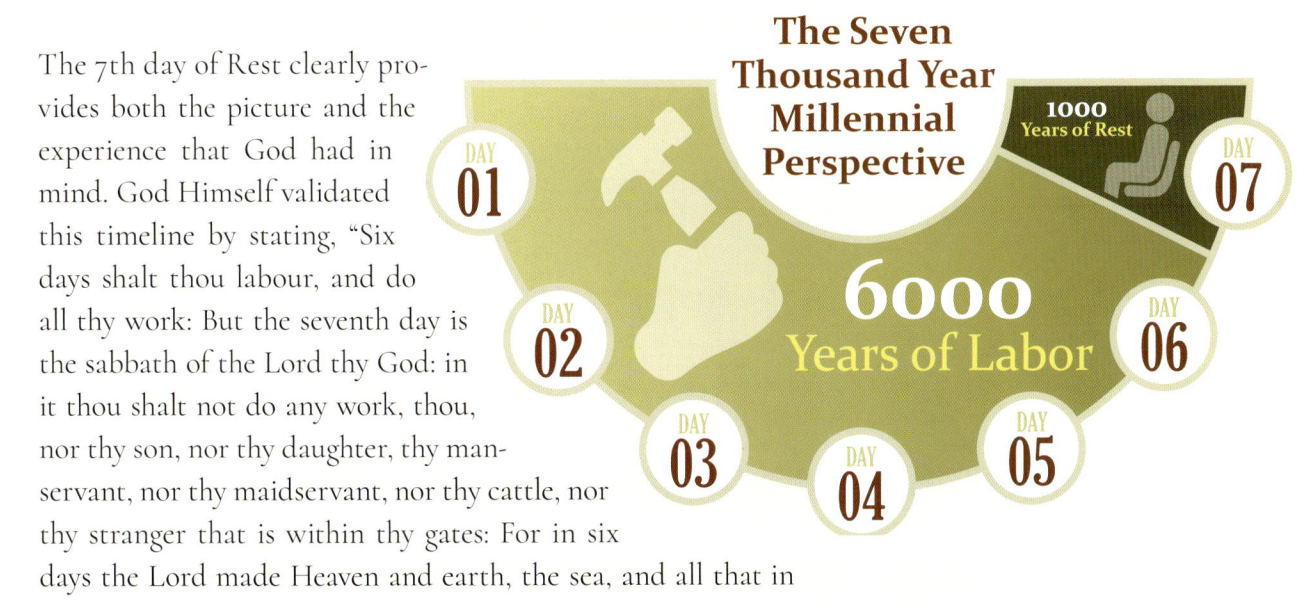

The 7th day of Rest clearly provides both the picture and the experience that God had in mind. God Himself validated this timeline by stating, "Six days shalt thou labour, and do all thy work: But the seventh day is the sabbath of the Lord thy God: in it thou shalt not do any work, thou, nor thy son, nor thy daughter, thy manservant, nor thy maidservant, nor thy cattle, nor thy stranger that is within thy gates: For in six days the Lord made Heaven and earth, the sea, and all that in them is, and rested the seventh day: wherefore the Lord blessed the sabbath day, and hallowed it."

God put man on a seven-day-cycle.

Why?

The mystery hidden in that daily cycle is rehearsed once a week.

Have you figured what is being rehearsed?

It should be plain to us, but often we miss it.

God is going to accomplish, in His time, the restoration of what man has so carelessly abandoned in the time he was given.

And what is it that God is going to restore in His perfect time?

The answer is astounding, humbling and surprising to anyone that understands what actually happened in the Garden of Eden.

God is communicating through His numbers that He has scheduled an appointed time in which He is going to restore His loving relationship with man.

The reversal of the curse was a planned appointed event on God's millennial calendar before the foundation of the world.

The entire revelation of God's Word from Genesis to Revelation is the seed plot that declares just how this reconciliation is going to take place.

God resting on the Seventh day of Creation.

Does God also reveal when all of this going to happen?

Are the clues hidden in plain sight everywhere you look in the revelation of the Beginning, the book of Genesis?

Is the First Clue in the First Week?

Is there a hidden prophetic harbinger in the cycle that begins with day one and ends every seventh day?

Every week of days is designed to come to a conclusion on the Sabbath or Seventh day.

Every time the Jews celebrate Shabbat, are they rehearsing a prophecy that ends with seven?

If so, what does God have planned for the Seventh Day?

The Scriptures give us the answer.

Each day is a prophetic harbinger of a thousand years.

Seven is the number of Divine Completion.

Do you know what God has scheduled for the final 7th day that God has determined to last 365,230 days or a thousand years?

What is scheduled on the prophetic timeline disclosed by the weekly 7-day cycle?

Is this a forecast of the ultimate timeline that God puts as a border and boundary around man's time of the earth?

If this is the correct outlook, then we should have evidence in the Scripture regarding the pivotal 7th day. The day God rested from His work. The day

Seven is the number of Divine Completion.

that we are to understand memorialized the ending of one thing and the beginning of something else, and then concludes the matter after 7000-years have been accomplished.

REVELATION 20:7

And when the thousand years are expired, Satan shall be loosed out of his prison.

REVELATION 21:1-4

And I saw a new Heaven and a new earth: for the first Heaven and the first earth were passed away; and there was no more sea.

And I John saw the holy city, new Jerusalem, coming down from God out of Heaven, prepared as a bride adorned for her husband.

And I heard a great voice out of Heaven saying, Behold, the tabernacle of God is with men, and he will dwell with them, and they shall be his people, and God himself shall be with them, and be their God.

And God shall wipe away all tears from their eyes; and there shall be no more death, neither sorrow, nor crying, neither shall there be any more pain: for the former things are passed away.

Has the Berisheet prophecy given us a clue as to when this is all going to happen?

Barnabas was not the first one to share the Sabbath Millennial Prophetic Perspective.

It was the belief of Saint Peter and it is highly unlikely that rest of the disciples of Jesus did not also share this outlook.

The 6000 Year Doctrine

Even those that do not adhere to the Sabbath-Millennial Prophetic Perspective admit that Jewish history supports what they call "the 6,000-year doctrine." The Sabbath-Millennial "doctrine" was considered established orthodoxy by many of the ancient Jewish Sages and Rabbis.

Today most of the Jewish Messianic believers, who go under the banner of Messianic Judaism, adhere to the 6000-year perspective, as did their ancient forefathers.

To be clear, this is the Millennial Outlook that allows 6000-years of human history corresponding to the six "days" (yomin) of Creation followed by a Seventh day or 1000-year period reserved for the Messiah and His 1000-year Millennial Kingdom.

To put this in an even wider historical perspective that Christians can have confidence in, it can be demonstrated that almost all the early church fathers (1st – 4th Century) held the Sabbath-Millennial Prophetic Perspective.

A brief history of the past is a good place to start considering the implications of the future.

To be clear, the Sabbath-Millennial eschatology is the most enduring and widely taught end-times outlook on earth. It was embraced by most of the early Christian Church Fathers.

This belief based on biblical literalism predicts that the time allowed for mankind is 7000 years and ends with fire.

> Most of the Jewish Messianic believers adhere to the 6000-year perspective.

It predicts that the 1000-year millennial reign of Jesus Christ from Jerusalem in Israel will take place immediately after the Second Coming of Christ at the end of the 6th millennium.

The Early Church Fathers vs Their Great, Great-Grandchildren

It is popular to quote the "early church fathers" against the "so-called" error of the pre-millennial eschatology.

What we discover upon investigation is what the "early church fathers" relied upon so heavily are actually later church great, great, great-grandchildren of the true early church fathers.

In modern parlance it would sort of be like consulting past President Bill Clinton as an authority on what happened at Independence Hall, Philadelphia in 1776, while ignoring the record and testimony of the founding fathers. Who is the most reliable source? Those that were actually there and their immediate descendants who would have been instructed by the founding fathers, or someone who shows up 200 years later?

If President Bill Clinton came up with a version of history that was at odds with the history preserved in the words and testimony of the founding fathers, would you give it any credence?

Of course not.

Why not?

Because not only was he not there and separated from the event by over 200 years but also because the actual founding fathers have recorded the events and there is absolutely no reason to doubt them.

Now compare this to the Millennial doctrine that was taught and believed by every major early church father going back to the Apostle John.

Apostle John the Theologian on the island of Patmos, Andrey Mironov, 2012.

Now imagine that this doctrine based on the foundational concept that the thousand-year reign of Christ was to be taken literally is being overthrown over 300 years later by late church grandchildren that have decided that what was good enough for Grandpa is not good enough for them.

History has taught us how rebellious great-grandchildren can be!

The bona-fide early church fathers were almost all millenialists (or chiliasts), as we will demonstrate in the next section of this book.

To be clear, what most of the popular and vocal opponents of Millennialism do not reveal is that almost all the teachings on eschatology from the "early church fathers" they so heavily relied upon have a start-date coincidental to the 4th century and Saint Augustine.

They ignore the early church fathers and relied on the grandchildren for their information.

Grandchildren that criticized their own fathers and grandfathers as they strayed from the original truth taught by the apostles including John the Revelator and St. Paul.

In other words, there is something basically disingenuous in the argument that the early church fathers starting with Augustine had abandoned the Sabbath Day Millennial prophetic perspective in favor of an allegorical non-literal interpretation of the Bible while ignoring the consistent millennial teachings in a straight line of succession up to the time of Augustine.

The insincerity of this is not lost on anyone who seriously studies church history. It is true that the millennial outlook was out of favor starting about the time that Constantine Christianized Rome in the 4th Century. This was soon followed by the novel biblical hermeneutics taught by St. Augustine.

Why would anyone give undue weight to the teaching of church leaders that were 300 years removed from the original Apostles, while slandering those that were taught by the Apostles and faithfully retained those teachings and

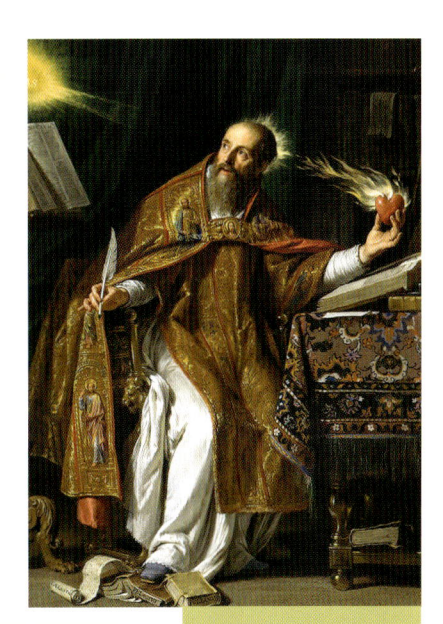

Saint Augustine by Philippe de Champaigne, 1648

doctrines until they were overthrown by the new non-literal method of biblical interpretation that was popularized by St. Augustine?

To make matters worse, the critics claim that there was a clamor against this "strange doctrine of millennialism" among many of the church fathers from Augustine forward. The impression is given that this was a battle against a heretical novel doctrine, when in fact they were the ones trying to overturn nearly three centuries of doctrine upheld and defended by a straight line of succession from the Apostle John.

The Battle for the Bible! Antioch vs. Alexandria

The battle in the 4th Century was not a battle over eschatology. It was a battle for the Bible. It was a battle for the literal interpretation of the Bible against an allegorical interpretation that ultimately leads to liberalism and unbelief. This is the root of the same "novel" perspective that has infected almost all modern-day Christendom.

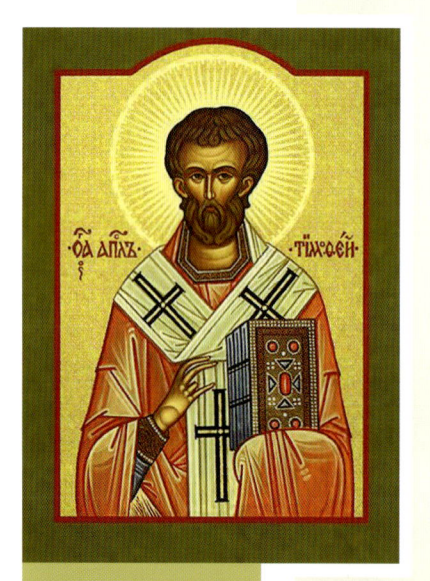

Leading up to the battle in the 4th Century (and beyond) was a competition between two schools of "thought" on biblical interpretation.

Out of Antioch (the place where the followers of Christ were first called "Christians") sprung a theological school of literal interpretation. This was "instruction" passed down from apostle to elder and so on, fulfilling Paul's directive in I Tim 2:2 (And the things that thou hast heard of me among many witnesses, the same commit thou to faithful men, who shall be able to teach others also). Paul taught Timothy, Timothy taught the elders, and these elders continued this tradition on.

Timothy of Lycaonian, was an early Christian evangelist and the first first-century Christian bishop of Ephesus.

Out of Alexandria, Egypt sprung a theological school influenced by Stoic philosophy and Platonism, mixed with the truths found in Christianity. The philosophers found it necessary to always find the allegorical meaning in a passage, as most of the philosophical literature at the time had highly immoral messages. So, in order to find the "good" in these passages, they were allegorized.

This tactic was taken on by the leaders in Alexandria such as Clement of Alexandria, Origen, Dionysius, and through the spread of early Christianity throughout North Africa, ultimately Augustine of Hippo builds on this platform and champions an allegorical view of the millennial reign, called "amillennialism," published in 426 AD in The City of God.

So, if you're going to rely on the early church fathers, doesn't it make some sense to go back as early as you can?

But of course, that would be embarrassing to the argument against millennialism and so they conveniently stop the research in the 4th Century AD. Or if the early church fathers are quoted, their "embarrassingly out-of-date and superstitious" belief about the millennium are conveniently removed from the discussion.

The simple truth that can be easily discovered by any serious student of church history is that the earliest church fathers retained a Sabbath Day Millennial viewpoint. Anyone that tells you different is guilty of creating a new biblical church fiction and is not reporting history as it actually happened.

The early Church Fathers were almost exclusively pre-millennialists. They proclaimed an end-times Gospel that included both the gathering of the glorified Church in the clouds and the Second Coming of Jesus our Lord. These two events were treated then as two separate events separated by a period of time of not less than 7 years.

Since Barnabas the Apostle has already been cited we will start our study with Justin Martyr.

Justin Martyr (100 – 165 AD)

Justin Martyr was also an apologist and defender of the Logos Christology. This is foundational for establishing the pre-existence and divinity of Jesus Christ, the second person in the Trinity.

Justin Martyr also taught the pre-millennial beliefs he received from John the Apostle. Justin Martyr cited the following verses as Scriptural proofs for his Sabbath Day Millennial beliefs.

Isaiah 65:17-25

For, behold, I create new Heavens and a new earth: and the former shall not be remembered, nor come into mind.

But be ye glad and rejoice forever in that which I create: for, behold, I create Jerusalem a rejoicing, and her people a joy.

And I will rejoice in Jerusalem, and joy in my people: and the voice of weeping shall be no more heard in her, nor the voice of crying.

There shall be no more thence an infant of days, nor an old man that hath not filled his days: for the child shall die an hundred years old; but the sinner being an hundred years old shall be accursed.

And they shall build houses, and inhabit them; and they shall plant vineyards, and eat the fruit of them.

They shall not build, and another inhabit; they shall not plant, and another eat: for as the days of a tree are the days of my people, and mine elect shall long enjoy the work of their hands.

They shall not labor in vain, nor bring forth for trouble; for they are the seed of the blessed of the Lord, and their offspring with them.

And it shall come to pass, that before they call, I will answer; and while they are yet speaking, I will hear.

The wolf and the lamb shall feed together, and the lion shall eat straw like the bullock: and dust shall be the serpent's meat. They shall not hurt nor destroy in all my holy mountain, saith the Lord.

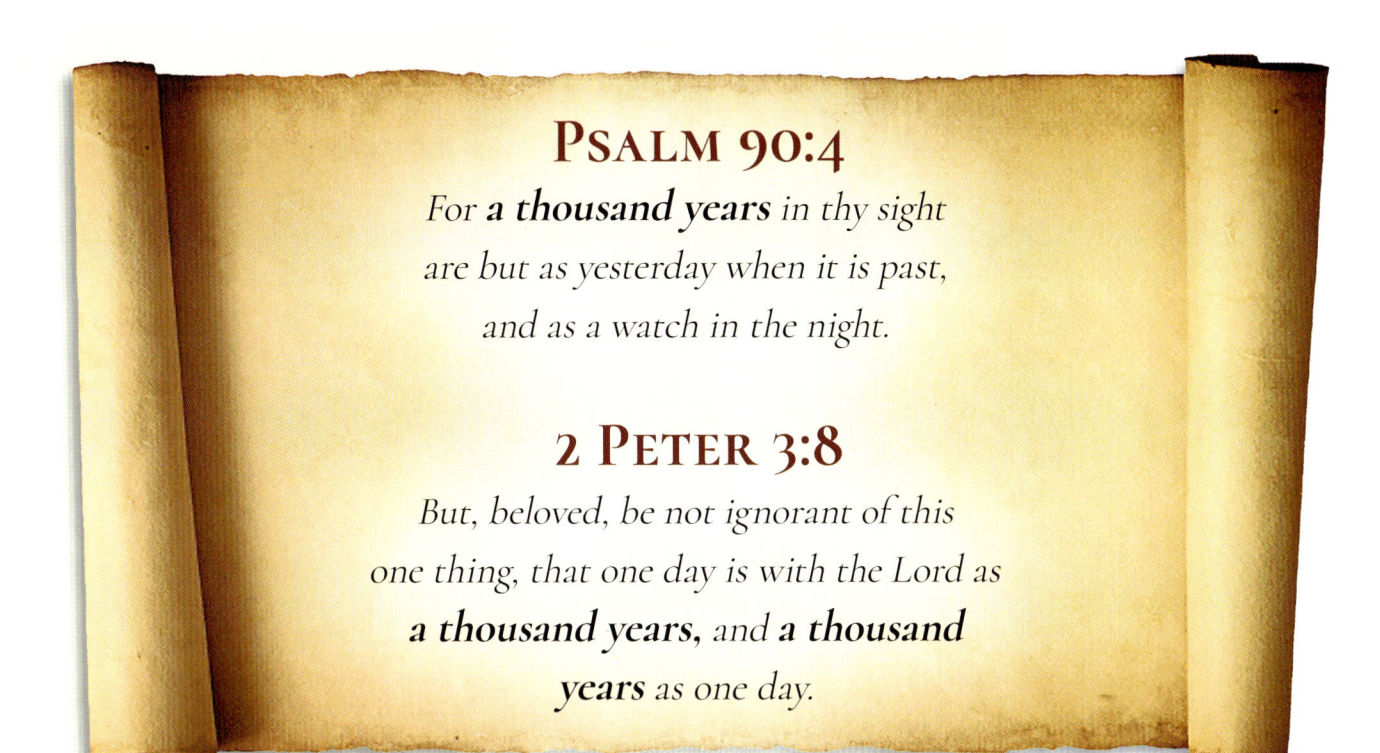

> ## Psalm 90:4
> For **a thousand years** in thy sight are but as yesterday when it is past, and as a watch in the night.
>
> ## 2 Peter 3:8
> But, beloved, be not ignorant of this one thing, that one day is with the Lord as **a thousand years,** and **a thousand years** as one day.

And, of course, Justin Martyr cited Revelation 20:1-7.

Papias (70 – 163 AD)

Although there are no surviving manuscripts of Papias' writings, his work is captured in writings of others. In Ecclesiastical History, Book 3 ca, Eusebius made mention of Papias (of whom he spoke very highly, except on this one particular point). He mentions how Papias was a disciple of John and Philip, the bishop of Hierapolis, and a friend of Polycarp.

Eusebius suggests that Papias actually wrote the Gospel of John at the dictation of John...so he was a man well-qualified to have an opinion on what the apostles taught.

Yet, Eusebius states, "he [Papias] says there would be a certain millennium after the resurrection, and that there would be a corporeal reign of Christ on this very earth; which things he appears to have imagined, as if they were authorized by the apostolic narrations, not understanding correctly those matters which they propounded mystically in their representations.

For he was very limited in his comprehension, as is evident from his discourses; yet he was the cause why most of the ecclesiastical writers, urging the antiquity of the man, were carried away by a similar opinion; as for instance, Irenaeus, or any other that adopted such sentiments."

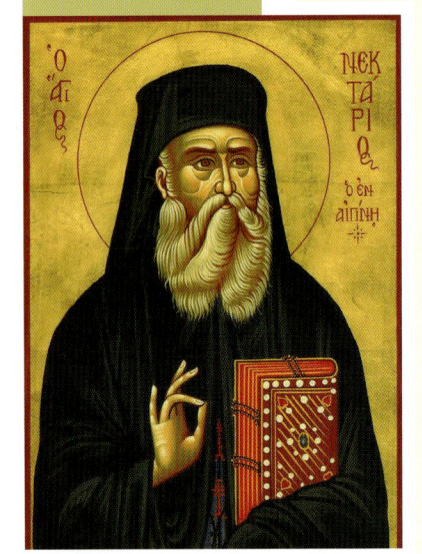

So out of Eusebius' own mouth, he contradicts his own "new Israel" view (amillennial) by stating that Papias was teaching the millennial reign as an apostolic narration, learned from the apostles and taught to others. Eusebius wrote these things nearly 300 years after the death of Christ. Once again, it would stand to reason that if Eusebius had a contention with Papias on what the apostles actually taught, that Papias would have a much clearer understanding of the topic given his proximity to the gospel writers.

If you want to know what the early church fathers taught regarding the end-times and the Second Coming of Jesus Christ, you need to look no further than the Sabbath Day Millennial perspective.

Irenaeus (130-202 AD)

Irenaeus was a famous church father and Bishop who could trace his doctrinal beliefs directly back to Polycarp, a disciple of Saint John the Apostle. Most historians also believe that Irenaeus was also a contemporary with the Apostle John.

Irenaeus taught that the Anti-Christ's future three-and-a-half year reign, when he sits in the temple at Jerusalem, would be terminated by the Second Coming of Christ.

Irenaeus taught that the Millennial Kingdom would be ruled by Jesus Christ for 1000 years followed by the general resurrection and the White Throne Judgment.

This would be followed by the fiery dissolution of the old earth at the end of the 7000-year millennium to be followed immediately by the Creation of a New Heaven and a New Earth.

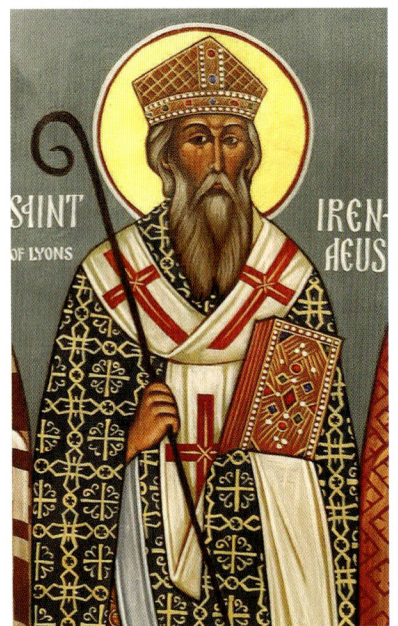

Irenaeus taught that the Millennial Kingdom was a literal, not an allegorical, kingdom.

Irenaeus held to the old Jewish tradition that the first six days of Creation week were a type of the first six thousand years of human history.

Although Irenaeus did have some novel ideas based on the traditions of the Jews that we might consider odd, his general view of things can be aptly described as a Sabbath Day Millennial outlook.

His best-known book is Against Heresies written in 180 AD. This book was a direct assault on the false teachings of the Gnostics.

Tertullian (155-240 AD)

Tertullian was a prolific writer in the northern Africa city of Carthage. In his treatise against Marcion, he writes, "But we do confess that a kingdom is promised to us upon the earth, although before Heaven, only in another state of existence; inasmuch as it will be after the resurrection for a thousand years in the divinely-built city of Jerusalem, 'let down from Heaven,' (Revelation 21:2) which the apostle also calls 'our mother from above;' (Galatians 4:26) and, while declaring that our πολίτευμα, or citizenship, is in Heaven, (Philippians 3:20) he predicates of it that it is really a city in Heaven. This both Ezekiel had knowledge of (Ezekiel 48:30-35) and the Apostle John beheld. (Revelation 21:10-23) And the word of the new prophecy which is a part of our belief, attests how it foretold that there would be for a sign a picture of this very city exhibited to view previous to its manifestation."

Now, Tertullian had some things wrong (e.g., he was convinced the new Jerusalem would descend in a particular area of Northern Africa; he later joined

Quintus Florens Tertullian, 160-220, church father and theologian

the Montanist movement out of frustration with the incorporation of philosophy into the teachings of scripture—a heretical movement incorporating female prophetess speaking "current revelation" from God, etc.), but when he says that "...we do confess..." he's not writing anything new—he's simply restating what the early church held to, which is the literal, millennial reign of Christ on earth.

Hippolytus of Rome (170 – 235 AD)

Hippolytus of Rome is considered by some students of church history to be one of the most important 3rd Century theologian in the Christian Church. Hippolytus was a disciple of Irenaeus who was a disciple of Polycarp who was a disciple of John the Apostle of Jesus Christ.

Hippolytus' most famous work is the Refutation of all Heresies.

Hippolytus is one of the first Christian teachers to emphasize end-times eschatology.

Hippolytus of Rome is considered one of the most important 3rd Century theologians in the Christian Church.

Hippolytus interpreted Daniel's seventy weeks as seventy prophetic weeks of literal years. This was not a novel idea but instead was the long-standing belief of all the church fathers that preceded him.

Hippolytus did not believe that the Second Coming of Christ was imminent.

The Second Coming that Hippolytus believed could be predicted based on the Sabbath-Millennial theory is not be confused with Christ's coming in the clouds to gather His church.

The date of the coming of Christ for the church was not in view in the forecast published by Hippolytus as it was distinct and separate from the Second Coming of Christ.

Hippolytus believed that the timing of Christ's Second Coming could be calculated. He assumed, as all the early church fathers that went before him did, that God created all things in six days. He believed that each day was emblematic of 1000 years.

Hippolytus predicted that Christ would come to set up His kingdom here on earth in the year 500 AD.

This erroneous calculation was based on the Septuagint's faulty chronology that the Creation of the world began in 5500 BC.

Did the Sabbath Day Millennial perspective fail?

Two errors contributed to the miscalculation of Hippolytus. The first error was the start-date of Creation that was off by 1500 years. Second, the erroneous idea that the 7 dispensations of 1000 years each would begin with Creation instead of the date of the fall of mankind through Adam.

Regardless of the erroneous end-dates, the position held by Hippolytus is that of the Sabbath Day Millennial and is again reflective of the teachings of the apostles and apostolic fathers.

Lactantius
(250 – 325 AD)

Lucius Lactantius was an early Church leader and author. He became an advisor to the first Christian Roman Emperor, Constantine I. Lactantius was responsible for overseeing the religious policy as it unfolded in the newly Christianized Roman Empire. Lactantius was also a tutor to Crispus the son of Constantine.

Like many of the early church fathers, Lactantius was a pre-millennialist, teaching that the second coming of Christ would precede a millennium or a thousand-year reign of Christ on earth. Lactantius in the early fourth century was determined to revive a more "genuine" form of chiliasm. Chiliasm is the Greek name for what we are calling the Sabbath Day Millennial Prophetic perspective.

> Lucius Lactantius, was a pre-millennialist, who taught that the second coming of Christ would precede a millennium or a thousand-year reign.

While most of the early church fathers up to the time of Augustine were pre-millennialist holding to the 7000-year theory, none was more voluminous on the topic than Lactantius.

Lactantius was a biblical literalist believing that the Sabbath Millennium would begin with the second advent of Christ.

Icon depicting Emperor Constantine, center, accompanied by the Church Fathers of the 325 First Council of Nicaea, holding the Nicene Creed in its 381 form.

Lactantius taught that Jesus would reign with the resurrected righteous on this earth during the seventh thousand years followed by the White Throne Judgment.

At the conclusion of this period Lactantius taught that Satan, having been bound during the thousand years, is released from his prison. Satan then mounts a worldwide rebellion against the righteous, who are hidden until the hosts, attacking the Holy City and are overwhelmed by fire and brimstone followed by a great earthquake.

God restores the earth and punishes the wicked. Finally, the Lord alone is worshipped in a renovated earth.

While this is not an exhaustive list of the early church fathers' opinions on this topic, what this should communicate is that the eschatology held by some of the earliest apostolic fathers is congruent with what the Bible teaches, and what most biblical literalists embrace to this day.

If you would like to read more about what the early church fathers taught, we would recommend the following books:

- *The Church from Conception to Misconception* by Buck Keely

- *Ancient Church Fathers – What the Disciples of the Apostles Taught* by Dr. Ken Johnson

Modern adherents have included Jerry Falwell, Tim LaHaye, Jerry Jenkins, Lester Sumrall and other well-known Bible scholars.

These and hundreds of others biblical literalists expected the millennial reign of Christ to begin in or around the year 2000 AD, believing that it marked the end of the 6000 years allotted to mankind.

CHAPTER 5

The First Two Beginnings

The Expulsion of Adam and Eve from Paradise, painting by Benjamin West, 1791.

Unfortunately, the ancient Sabbath-Millennial Prophetic Perspective is out of favor with a growing number of Christians today.

The reason for this is pretty simple.

The Sabbath Day Millennial outlook, based on a start-date of Creation in 4004 BC "seems" to have failed.

I would like to propose that the reason for the apparent failure of the Sabbath Day Millennium theory has nothing to do with any deficiency in the 7000-year prophetic period being forecast.

Missing the Mark

The libraries of the world are filled with fictional narratives based on the adventures that unfold while searching for lost treasure.

The key seed plot that undergirds many of these stories is something I call the Mystery of the Missing X.

Chapters are devoted to the mystery surrounding the starting point of the treasure map, the missing location of the X. Finding the treasure is the final act; the bulk of the storyline is pre-occupied with the discovery of the Missing X.

The missing X is almost always found in the last chapter of the book.

This crucial clue is usually written on a small scrap of parchment that has been carefully torn from the treasure map and secreted away in some unknown spot.

Clues as to where this missing X is hidden abound, but only the wise and persistent ultimately prevail in discovering the mystery of the missing X and all the treasure it promises to the persistent searcher.

In other words, without the right starting point, you will never find the treasure.

It is all about the starting point.

Have we missed the Precise Center Point?

If the starting point is missed then obviously the entire prophetic perspective is nothing more than just another unsolved mystery.

The mistaken idea that the start-date for the Sabbath Day Millennial system began with the first day of Creation has been proven unreliable.

We are now left with several options.

We can abandon the most revered and ancient prophetic outlook to ever be seriously considered by those that take the Bible literally.

We can torture the calendar until it comes up with some more missing time.

Or, we are left to re-test and re-think all our presuppositions. This would include renewing the rigor with which we interpret Scriptures literally.

The Sabbath Day Millenial prophetic outlook is seriously considered by those that take the Bible literally.

Without the right start-date, nothing works out as expected, creating disappointment from those that relied upon it, and skepticism from all those that are looking for any excuse to ridicule and dismiss anything to do with biblical prophecy.

And isn't that exactly what has happened over the last 2000 years?

Disappointment has resulted from the missed target dates proposed by those that used the Sabbath Day Millennium theory in order to forecast the Second Coming of Christ. Some notable and respected early church fathers who thought they were living 5500 years from the start-date of Creation even ventured to make predictions based on the Day for a Thousand Years perspective. And of course, were ultimately proven wrong.

104 | THE BERISHEET END-TIMES PASSOVER PROPHECY
C.J. LOVIK

Untold numbers of Christians through the ages have been disappointed when the latest prophetic outlook based on the 6000 years for man perspective didn't result in the 2nd Coming of Christ!

Cults have risen from the seeds of prophecy forecasters that got it wrong but could not admit their error. Errors which they compounded with a ready supply of false teaching and doctrine to keep the "faithful" from drifting off the reservation.

The entire Sabbath Day Millennial Prophecy historically and currently rests on the start-date of the Creation of the World.

The Mystery Of the Two Dispensations!

The first hint that there might be a problem with this perspective is that the Creation Start-Date ends up including two distinct and mutually exclusive dispensations of time.

What are these two over-arching dispensations?

The Bible clearly spells them out.

The first dispensation of Innocence begins with Genesis 1:1 and ends abruptly in Genesis 3:6;

GENESIS 3:6

And when the woman saw that the tree was good for food, and that it was pleasant to the eyes, and a tree to be desired to make one wise, she took of the fruit thereof, and did eat, and gave also unto her husband with her; and he did eat.

The beginning of the second dispensation of Sin and Rebellion is reported in Genesis 3:7 and comes to a climax as reported in the book of Revelation 21:27:

> **REVELATION 21:27**
> *And there shall in no wise enter into it anything that defileth, neither whatsoever worketh abomination, or maketh a lie: but they which are written in the Lamb's book of life.*

In a nutshell, there are two over-arching dispensations based on the condition of the heart of man and his relationship to his Creator.

One dispensation unfolds over days, weeks, and years.

The other transpires over millennia.

Obviously, there are other dispensations (economies) that occur sequentially within the Dispensation of Sin and Rebellion.

The basic fundamental difference between the two dispensations that over-arch everything from the Creation of Adam and Eve to the Creation of a new Heavens and Earth is not hard to figure out.

One dispensation was marked by the absence of sin.

The other dispensation has been marked by the overflowing presence of sin.

The age of innocence in which man was sinless and not sinning bears no resemblance to the dispensation of time in which man is a sinner who is continually and habitually sinning.

Even with the apparent failure of the Sabbath Day Millennial theory, most people have either abandoned the concept or are still holding on to the start-date of Creation.

Dispensationalist are always focused on "rightly dividing the word of truth." But apparently the combination of two polar opposite dispensations resulting in a time-stamp forecast that should have climaxed with the 2nd Coming of Christ sometime between 1996 – 2000 AD has escaped their notice.

Using the start-date of Creation and adding 6000 years produces a date that has come and gone.

The year 1995-1996 would be exactly 6000 years since Creation based on a start date of 4004 BC.

Either the Sabbath Day Millennium outlook has failed or it is about to unfold in this generation based on a time-frame and a start-date that we have overlooked.

What's missing?

The right start-date!

Things that are not the same are different!

I believe that the start-date for the Sabbath Day Millennial prophecy began the day that Adam sinned.

Foundational to the search for a new start-date based on the sin of Adam is the belief that the Sabbath Day Millennial theory is a prophecy that includes sinful man only and does not include the "Dispensation of Innocence" when Adam lived a perfect life in the Garden of Eden.

I believe this is a reasonable presupposition.

Time will tell!

This theory and its amazing implication is the intriguing subject of this book.

CHAPTER 6

4004 BC
The Date of Creation?

Creation of the Sun, Moon, and Planets, fresco by Michelangelo, 1511.

As of 2018, we are living 6022 years from the proposed Creation date of 4004 BC.

> ## Isaiah 46:9-10
> *Remember the former things of old: for I am God,*
> *and there is none else;*
> *I am God, and there is none like me,*
> *Declaring the end from the beginning,*
> *and from ancient times the things that are not yet done, saying,*
> *My counsel shall stand, and I will do all my pleasure:*

4004 BC CREATION

The reader may be interested in how I arrived at the year of 4004 as the Creation date.

Anyone familiar with Biblical Chronology is familiar with Bishop James Ussher, who "reckoned" that the Creation of the world took place in the year 4004 BC based on a literal reading of the chronology of the Old and New Testament.

Bishop Ussher is often a figure to be ridiculed in our age of anti-supernatural consciousness informed and governed by the modern theories of cosmology and anthropology.

Modern theories date our world with a generous helping of zeroes that take us back to epochs and ages that no man can actually comprehend. These epochs of time provide a large canvas with wide borders. These "forever and ever" boundaries, as it turns out, are needed in order to produce insanely complex cosmological math equations. Any research into this subject unveils the truth that it is all rooted in fanciful theories, not on honest inquiry and investigation.

Chalk, as it turns out, is the best metaphor for the entire enterprise as it is published and then almost immediately turned into dust as the next best and newest theory clamors for its turn on the big black or blue dusty board.

Bishop Ussher and the Beginning of Creation!

Compare this to the lifetime work of Dr. James Ussher, one of the most careful, rational and intelligent scholars to live on this earth in the last 350 years.

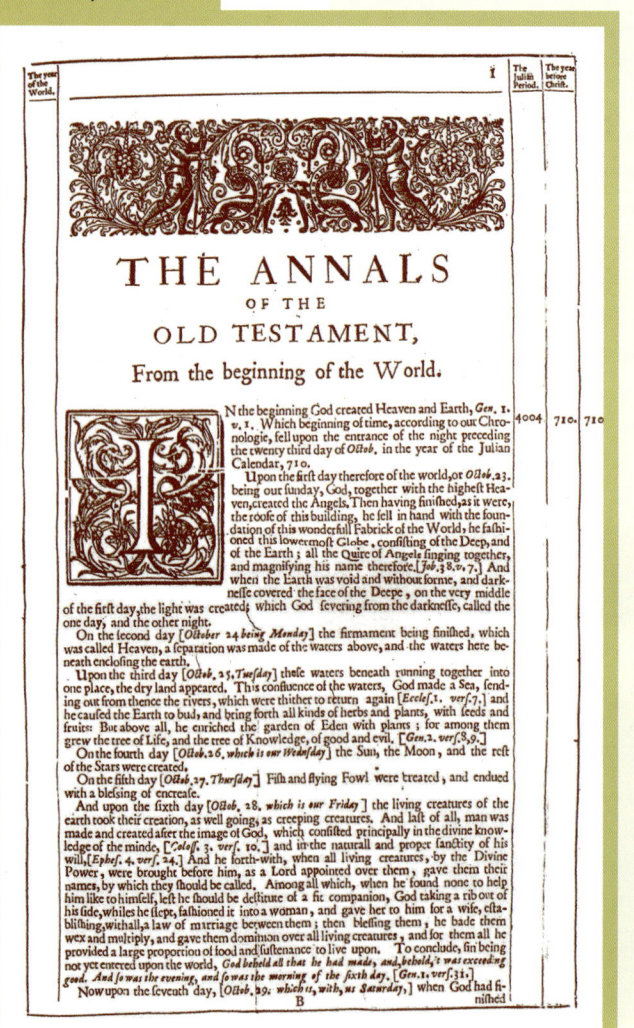

Bishop Ussher devoted his life to the careful production of the chronology of the ancient world, producing a work of 2000 pages titled Annals of the World, commonly known as *The Annals*.

Ussher's chronology spanned a period of time between the Creation of the World and the Destruction of the Jewish Temple in 70 AD.

James Ussher did not use a blackboard to come to his conclusions. Dr. Ussher traveled throughout all Europe ferreting out information from original historical documents, many of which have been destroyed since the time of his research.

The Annals of history rewards the patient reader with an insightful and sometimes surprising history of the ancient world.

Bishop Ussher died at the age of 75 and was buried at the insistence of Cromwell in the chapel of St Erasmus in Westminster Abbey. This is a testimony to how highly regarded Bishop Ussher was by his peers and countrymen.

Annals of the World, page 1, author James Ussher, 1658.

Bishop Ussher is not the only serious biblical chronologist who has arrived at the Creation date of 4004. Careful biblical research aided by the advances in computational technology has led to several serious attempts to date Creation.

This has resulted in several confirming witnesses to the 4004 BC date of Creation.

I began this small article with a question.

How did I arrive at the biblical six-day Creation date of 4004 BC?

Did I spend years researching the work of Bishop Ussher whose original work written in Latin has recently been republished and translated into English? Or perhaps I have been studying any one of the many works that have been done on this topic?

Note that there have been over 100 independent research projects producing books and articles that all roughly confirm the amazing accuracy of Bishop Ussher's Biblical chronology.

Perhaps I took a shortcut and in a blind leap of faith, did I just copy and paste the headlines of my favorite Biblical Chronologist and come up with 4004 BC?

The truth of the matter is much more interesting and provocative.

HOW DID I arrive at the Creation Date of 4004 BC?

James Ussher, painting by Cornelis Janssens van Ceulen, 1641.

The Answer

The calculation is not difficult and does not require that you consult the vast amount of chronological information revealed in the Scripture. My calculation rests on ONE biblical revelation disclosed in Genesis 1:1 that has been confirmed by the most notable and talked about event to ever take place in history.

This ONE chronological event is the Center Point of all man's history and provides an overview that spans the entire 7000 years that God has put on His millennial calendar for man.

> **1** The One Event is the Epic Sacrifice made by the Son of God on Mt. Moriah in the city of Jerusalem in 30 AD.

The second chronological event that is a consequence of the ONE Event in view and provides the one puzzle piece that allows us to accurately date the start date which spans the entire 7000 years that God has put on His millennial calendar for sinful man.

Incarnation, painting by Piero di Cosimo, earlier than 1584.

> **2** The Second Event is the miracle of the Incarnation of Jesus Christ that took place in 4 BC.

This provides a time span of thirty-three plus an unknown exact number of months (between the birth of Jesus in 4 BC and His atoning death in 30 AD).

> **3** The ONE Biblical Revelation is the Berisheet Prophecy, the first prophecy in the Bible. This prophetic perspective reveals a 4000 year time-span that looks back from the Crucifixion event of 30 AD, an event it both forecasts and provides a time-stamp from which all the other events can be easily calculated in real time.

With these three puzzle pieces we can now date both Creation and the one date that has eluded discovery up until now. The date that Adam sinned. The date that ended the sinless 33 years in the Garden of Eden and inaugurated the 7000 years millennial countdown to the end of this present world. Remember, this can shift by up to 5 years depending on the date Jesus died on the cross, which could be a couple years earlier or later than the date of 30 AD that we are using in order to demonstrate the Berisheet End-Times Passsover Prophecy time line.

Ussher's "get er done" Blunder

Ussher proposed that Adam was created, named all the animals, was introduced to Eve and ate the forbidden fruit all on the very first seven days of the creation narrative.

While this speculation seems unreasonable, and unlikely, it is what Bishop Ussher taught. This idea is even held by some Christians to this day.

All concepts have consequences and this particular novel idea had a concept that corrupted the Sabbath Day Millennial theory for hundreds of years.

Adam and Eve in Paradise, painting by Johann Wenzel Peter, before 1829.

The basic problem with Bishop Ussher's conclusion is that it dates the fall of Adam and the Creation of the earth within a period of one literal week without any biblical warrant.

So, if you ever entertained the notion that the start-date for the millennial perspective should start with the sin of Adam instead of the start of Creation, the difference in time being only one week was not worth reckoning or debating.

It was Bishop Ussher's confidence in that date and the Sabbath Day Millennial theory that prompted him in the 17th century to predict that the Second Coming of Christ would take place on October 23, 1996 AD.

Bishop Ussher calculated that 1996 was exactly 6000 years from Creation. This was based on his 4004 BC Creation of the world date that I believe is correct. Even with a correct start-date based on the Creation of the world, the prediction was still doomed to fail.

Bishop Ussher is now on a long list of "discredited date setters." He is not treated as badly by history as those predicting dates based on secret messages from alien life-forms, or calculating the coming of Christ based on the dimensions of Noah's ark.

But he was still wrong.

Now that we have exposed the flaws of Bishop Ussher, let's consider his masterful and lifelong scholarly work of bringing the literal chronology of the Bible and overlaying with amazing precision over the Gregorian Calendar that we rely upon to this day.

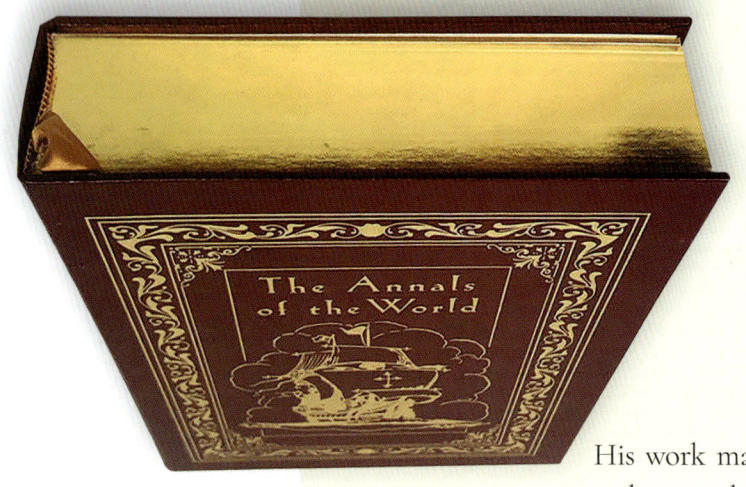

Bishop Ussher laid the groundwork for the chronological and literal understanding of the Scriptures. The huge gaps in time that went unnoticed, resulting in speculation that was off in some cases by over a thousand years that were rooted in translation errors in the Septuagint, ended after Bishop Ussher published his monumental work.

His work may not have been perfect, but it was ultimately proved to be surprisingly accurate. A progression of over 100 scholars have also taken it upon themselves to discover the timelines of the Bible and correlate it to our current calendar. Many of the modern works have been rather recent and aided by computer technology. All have basically come to the conclusion that the general time-line proposed by Ussher was close to the mark.

To be clear, we can know with a high degree of certainty that based on a literal interpretation of the Bible the year 1996-2000 AD marked the six-thousandth year from Creation.

Although it was not the start-date for the Sabbath Day Millennial theory as proposed by Ussher and others, it was nonetheless a start-point that could be relied upon with some degree of confidence.

Anyone that is trying to figure out what happened and when it happened in the Bible is probably looking at a timeline that owes much of the amazing accuracy to the tenacity and scholarship of Bishop Ussher and those that followed in his footsteps.

This is important because the premise of this book is that the incorrect dating of the Second Coming of Christ based on the Sabbath Day Millennium perspective failed because the start-date was simply in error.

To suggest that the Sabbath Day Millennium prophecy failed cannot be known because the terminal date of this prophecy has not been reached nor will it be until the year 2030 AD, give or take a couple years.

The Berisheet Prophecy does not start with the Creation date but provides us with a new start-date from which to lay down our millennial ruler. Instead of guessing about all the possible ways the calendar could have been corrupted since Creation, or even since the sin of Adam, we are given a reset date from which to measure time based on a much more recent event, the Crucifixion of Christ in 30 AD, less than 2000 years ago. Clearly our ability to rightly reckon the time left on God's millennial calendar has been made much easier.

Bible primer, Old Testament, illustration by Adolph Hult, 1919.

Clearly what caused the failure was not the 6000 year time sequence but the start-date and the erroneous speculation that Adam sinned on the 7th day of Creation.

Happily, for Bishop Ussher, the date he predicted was so far into the future that he suffered no personal loss of prestige or the rude mockery of skeptics as a result of his failed prediction.

One lesson of end-times date setting seems to be that it is better not to be around to see the prediction fail. Not being alive on the scene when your prophecy fails does have its advantages.

The good Bishop Ussher is now in Heaven waiting for the event he miss-calculated to finally manifest in time and space. Is he feeling bad? NO WAY!

Ironically his failure does not diminish the fact that God used Bishop Ussher in order to give us confidence that God's timeline for mankind was clearly unfolded in the sacred Scriptures.

Obviously, the prediction regarding the Second Coming of Christ made by James Ussher was delivered sincerely with no expectation of personal profit and without malice.

If anyone had paid the price demanded by good scholarship with the resources available to him in the 17th Century it was Bishop Ussher. And yet the good bishop offers up a prediction that not only fails but inspires others to follow and fail as well.

His problem was not sincerity.

His problem was an unwarranted certainty regarding a matter that requires humility as a standard against presumptuousness.

Those that mock Bishop Ussher and his conclusions would be hard pressed to match his intellect and broad knowledge of history.

The lesson in humility still remains. He might have been more easily forgiven for his error had he been more careful in how he presented his conclusions.

As we said earlier, many biblical researchers reached the same conclusion as Bishop Ussher while some biblical researchers, building on Ussher's scholarship, calculated that the world was created in the zero year and calculated from **1 Anno Mundi** (calculation based on a start-date from the Creation of the earth). This would be 4004, the first year of Creation based on the Julian calendar. A few have produced theories based on the biblical and historical record that the Creation date could be off by as much as 110 years.

The belief predicated on biblical literalism predicts that the time allowed for mankind is 7000 years beginning with a start-date of Creation. The 7000 years or seventh millennium ends with the destruction of the earth by fire and the Creation of a new Heaven and a new Earth.

The Berisheet End-Times Passover Prophecy forecast that the end of our present Heaven and Earth is appointed to take place 3000 years from the year Christ was crucified in 30 AD.

I mention this again as my second reminder that we need not depend upon the start-date of Creation since God has pinpointed the one date, the exact year that all time prophecies related to the Second Coming of Christ and the end of the present world will take place. The center point of all the future events is directly connected to the event that took place on Mt. Moriah in 30 AD, give or take a couple of years.

Chapter 7

How Long was Adam in the Garden?

We have already learned that the Berisheet End-Times Passover Prophecy allows us to make an educated guess as to how long Adam was in the Garden before sin entered the world. The educated guess is based on a larger-than-life, convincing prophetic pattern.

Is this a coincidence?

Perhaps, but I doubt it.

Is it possible that Adam lived in the Garden for more than 33 years before he sinned?

Of course, it is possible but unlikely based on the prophetic patterns of Scripture.

To be clear, the Berisheet End-Times Passover Prophecy does not rely upon the start-date of Creation, but rather points us to the start-date for Adam's sin and rebellion.

Are there clues in the biblical narrative that give us the possible window of time in which the seditious act of Adam could have taken place?

Does our prophetic date fit into the boundaries of the biblical narrative?

The answer is *yes*.

In order to bolster the conclusion of the Berisheet End-Times Passover Prophecy that forecasts a 3970 BC start-date for sin and rebellion, let's see if we can glean from the Scriptures anything that either supports or denies this conclusion.

Remember that the Berisheet End-Times Passover Prophecy does not forecast the start-date for Creation, but the start date for Sin and Rebellion. The start-date for Creation is "surmised" based on the window of time between the Creation of Adam and the sin of Adam.

The window of time in which Adam could have sinned could not have been more than 100 years. (Based on the age of 130 with the birth of Seth--less 30 years, the estimated age of Cain when he slew Abel--plus the time in between those two events.)

The Day the Earth Changed!

It happened so quickly he could hardly catch his breath.

In an instant it was over!

The succulent juice from the fruit dripped off his chin and landed on the ground with a chilling clap.

The light that had just moments before brightened his soul, dimmed and finally vanished.

No longer clothed with luminous light, Adam glanced down in shock.

His very first thoughts of unworthiness were so gripping that he fell to his knees and covered his eyes.

What was this overwhelming, crushing conviction he suddenly felt?

Shame had entered the garden.

He cringed holding himself tightly, bowed with the stabbing spasm in his chest and stomach.

Pain had entered the garden.

He slowly opened his eyes with his jaw clinched hoping the nightmare would pass.

It did not.

The heart of Adam was in one terrible instant, broken. This breach left a chasm so deep as it severed the bonds of love and fellowship between himself and his Creator, Elohim.

Sin had invaded the Garden of Eden.

It was a day Adam would never forget, nor should we.

It was a terrible day that seems to be lost in time.

The prologue to this chapter is a fictionalized version of the very real events that sent mankind headlong into a world of thistles, thorns, toil and sorrow.

The sad day that sin and rebellion ended the promise of Eden.

None of our calendars memorialize this event. Yet, it is the most horrific tragic day in the history of mankind. It is a day unequaled in its significance, perhaps only to the death of the Christ of God on the cross. It is a day that is conspicuous in its absence from the history books or almanacs that chronicle every sort of misery but fail to ever mention the one event that is responsible for all the wars, disease, sickness and death not to mention the groaning of the earth itself resulting in earthquakes, fires, tornadoes, tsunamis, floods, pestilence, and a thousand other miseries.

Adam and Eve Chased out of the Terrestrial Paradise, painting by Jean-Achille Benouville, 1841

It is the day when paradise was banished from everything except the corrupted imagination and corrupted memories of mankind.

It is the first of many horrific days that were now destined to follow one after another in a parade of sorrows that would go on until it reached the end.

This tragic day should be the headline banner that introduces the ever-growing chronicles of catastrophes.

Sadly, it is not!

It is the lost day.

A day that goes unnoticed and unheeded.

Adam's SIN-DAY

Celebrated the world over in every moment of every day in every man and women's life since the fall of Adam.

It is much more than curiosity that propels this inquiry into the year that Adam was expelled from the Garden of Eden.

Could it be that correctly calculating the year that Adam sinned would provide the one missing puzzle piece needed to discover the seasons of man that mark both the beginning and the end declared by God in Isaiah 46—the beginning and the end of a 7000-year saga?

When did the floodgates of sin and hell burst forth into the domain of mankind carrying Adam and all his descendants away in a tsunami of spiritual and physical death and destruction?

When will it all come to an end?

The warning to avoid one forbidden tree, standing alone and solitary, is now multiplied as we see before us forests full of tempting trees laden with the low-hanging forbidden fruit of sin and iniquity.

The Fields are Ripe with the Noxious and Toxic Fruit of Rebellion

We can now roam orchards full of every variety of sin and rebellion stretching before us as far as the eye can see. These groves all bear the same poisonous and corrupt fruit of lies, lust and lunacy.

In a word, the bad fruit that always springs up from sedition and rebellion is now the "fruit de-jour."

There is no question that Adam's sin marked a new and sad beginning for both himself and all his descendants, including each one of us.

Again, we ask, when did this all of this happen?

How long were Adam and Eve in the Garden of Eden before they were evicted?

When was the doorway that led back into the Garden of Eden slammed shut and guarded by fiery swords and celestial gatekeepers?

Is it just curiosity, an unwarranted probing into things just outside the bounds of what is knowable?

I believe that the answer to this question is no!

The Bible is full of mysteries.

One of the first mysteries we encounter in God's Word relates to time and how it is reckoned and purposed by both God and man.

Clearly God wants us to understand that He created the world in six literal, 24-hour days.

God wants us to understand why the world we now live in is not the world Adam and Eve initially inhabited.

God Judging Adam, painting by William Blake, 1795.

Time that was once a Treasure is Now a Ticking Time Bomb!

The mystery of time was transformed from existential bliss to a ticking time bomb of death and destruction. It all happened in one split second of time, one solitary moment, from man's perspective.

From God's perspective, the purpose of time was not refashioned. God was using time to test man.

Man failed the test of time.

If Adam was being tested, and it seems obvious that he was, how long was the test under the most ideal circumstance possible, designed originally to last?

The answer is not clear.

The clues we are given only allow us to make an educated guess.

There would have been no precedent that would allow us to know the answer to this question at the moment Adam fell into sin. But there are some well-marked clues with historical precedent as we look back in time at this tragic event.

The Number 40 and What It Means

The only clues we have are based on God's revelation as it has unfolded over time. This disclosure allows us to make an educated guess that the period of probation in the Garden of Eden was connected to the number forty.

Did you know that forty is the last number in Adam's name?

Was Adam to be tested forty years in the Garden of Eden?

Who was tested 40 days in the Judean wilderness?

Remember that Pattern is Prophecy.

MARK 1:13

And he was there in the wilderness forty days, tempted of Satan; and was with the wild beasts; and the angels ministered unto him.

Can we speculate that Adam had been given a 40 year period of testing and was therefore in the Garden for less than 40 years?

Is this a reasonable presupposition?

Before you decide, look at the Picture and Number clues embedded in the name of ADAM.

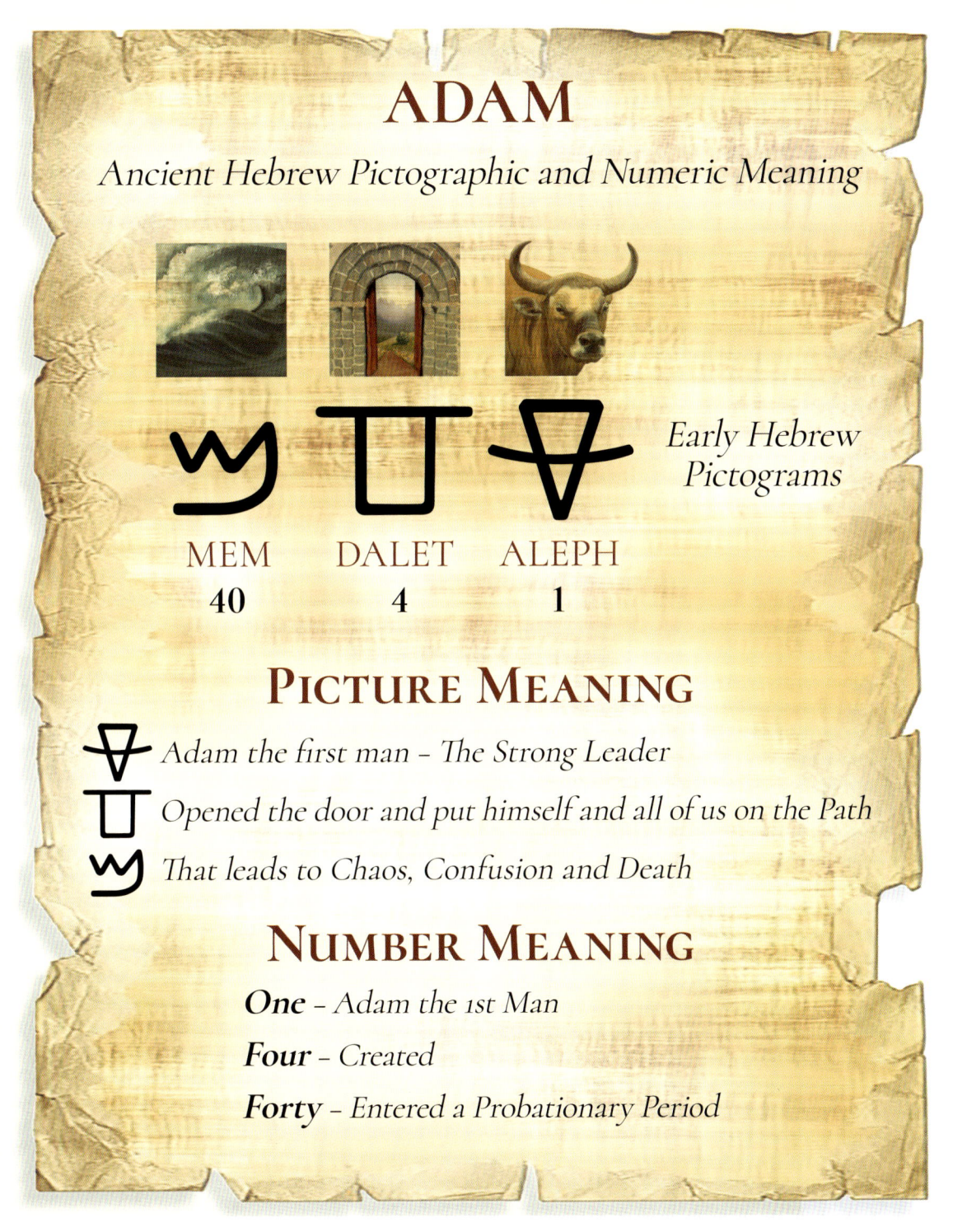

ADAM
Ancient Hebrew Pictographic and Numeric Meaning

Early Hebrew Pictograms

MEM	DALET	ALEPH
40	4	1

Picture Meaning

Adam the first man – The Strong Leader

Opened the door and put himself and all of us on the Path

That leads to Chaos, Confusion and Death

Number Meaning

One – Adam the 1st Man

Four – Created

Forty – Entered a Probationary Period

THE BERISHEET END-TIMES PASSOVER PROPHECY
CHAPTER 7: HOW LONG WAS ADAM IN THE GARDEN?

Let's tuck that insight into our journal and move ahead with our hunt to try and calculate the wideness of the window of time in which the sad genesis of sin made its calamitous entry.

We clearly understand the event that resulted in Adam being cast out of the Garden of Eden, but are we any closer to understanding how long Adam and Eve were in the Garden of Eden?

One way of calculating the general time-frame would be to find the first biblically dated event that happened in the lifetime of Adam.

We know that Adam lived to be 930 years old.

What other dates does the Bible connect to Adam?

We know that Adam and Eve had two sons outside the Garden of Eden.

Their names were Cain and Abel, and, unfortunately, we we are not given the year they were born.

Were they twins born in the same year?

We simply do not know.

After Cain fled his home to wander on the earth and Abel's blood cried out from the ground, another son was born to Adam and Eve.

The Appointed Son
The Type of Messiah

GENESIS 5:3
And Adam lived a hundred and thirty years, and begat a son in his own likeness, and after his image; and called his name Seth:

Using common sense as our guide, we can speculate that Cain was a young adult when he killed his brother Abel.

How old was he?

We simply do not know but we can make a conservative guess that Cain was no younger than 20 years old.

It is probable then that we can date the exit from the Garden no later than 110 years after Creation.

Is this as close as we can get without speculating?

Is there another Clue in EDEN?

Let's look at this question from another point of view.

What was God's purpose of putting Adam and Eve in the Garden of Eden?

Could the answer be hidden in plain sight in the name of Eden?

Although this is speculative and admittedly a rabbit trail, it may provide some unexpected insight into the question and add some credibility to the speculation that Adam was in the Garden to be tested for 40 years. A test Adam fell seven years short of passing.

Seven years?

Isn't that interesting?

> **GENESIS 2:8**
> And the Lord God planted a garden eastward in Eden; and there he put the man whom he had formed.

Have you wondered what Eden was all about?

Let's take a look at the Hebrew word Eden and see if it yields up any interesting clues as to the tenure of Adam in the Garden that God planted east of Eden.

EDEN
What Does the Picture of Eden Reveal?

NOON	DALET	AYIN
50	4	70

70 To See – To Know – To Experience

4 Pathway – Doorway – Gate – Place of Decision
Entrance to Life or Death – Moving into something
Moving out of something – To Open up
A Place where Change can take place – Door

50 Activity – Life
50 Noon
Holy Spirit – Pentecost – Deliverance
Followed by Rest – Grace Multiplied
JUBILEE

THE PICTURE MEANING OF EDEN

To Experience Entering the Path that Leads to Eternal Life. The picture meaning is amplified by the number meaning of Noon. The number 50 is the number of multiplied grace, deliverance and the gracious work of the Holy Spirit. It is the number connected to Deliverance, JUBILEE!

The picture is also magnified by the meaning of the three numbers in the Hebrew word Eden. Noon summarizes the numeric revelation. It is about deliverance and grace.

Deliverance followed by Rest
JUBILEE

What Door will our Leader Open?

Will Adam pass the test and enter the doorway that leads to eternal rest?

Let's go back to the mini-age of innocence as we watch with renewed interest. Everything now appears to be moving toward a climax that will culminate in a glorified body that will never sin or die.

And then, in one instant of time, the whole drama changes from bright and hopeful to gloom, doom and despair.

The one thing the Creator forbade has now become the delight of the creatures.

In one second, one mouth dripping with the poisonous venom of the forbidden fruit has chased away the light and exchanged it for the darkest of all nights.

The truth cannot be denied or hidden as Adam stands naked and ashamed midst the garden of probation.

Adam has made his choice. And he made his choice not just for himself. Adam made the choice for all his descendants. He made the choice for all of us.

The doorway and the path that leads to life eternal has been shunned in favor of the door that leads to chaos, confusion and death. Eden's doorway is no longer on the earth.

For one brief moment, we hear a hissing sound that echoes throughout the Garden. It is the hideous chortling of the self-satisfied serpent.

We are not surprised that Adam and his helpmate, Eve, are driven out of the Garden of Eden. We view with sadness as our first parents venture into a harsh world filled with as many unpleasant surprises as there were secret delights in the Garden of Eden.

But before we leave the Garden, there is one last encounter with the Creator within the boundaries of the garden of probation.

One Small Hopeful Sign!

There is also one hopeful sign that is the precursor to the last garden conversation between man and his Creator.

Our adversary, Satan, was created perfect and without defect until iniquity entered his heart. Filled with pride, he imagined himself equal to God. This vainly imagined equality was laden with malice.

To add insult to the folly, Satan foolishly imagined that God was capable of the same petty jealousies and insecurities that had taken root in his own withered heart.

Obsessed by the fever that now piloted his mind, Satan began to maliciously slander the Creator, a pattern of behavior that has continued to this very day.

Satan, illustration for the book Paradise Lost, Gustave Dore, 1866.

Satan's slanderous and malicious misrepresentations of God were contagious. It soon took root in the minds of other created angelic beings.

Before long, a third of Heaven's hosts were infected with the rebellious, greedy, self-elevating, and vain spirit that first darkened Satan's mind and heart.

It should come as no surprise that this rebellion resulted in Satan being removed from his glorified position of preferment and cast out of Heaven's dominion except as noted in Scripture.

(Satan the slanderer is constantly acting as a prosecuting attorney in the courts of Heaven where he is allowed to bring his accusations against the saints of God. This privilege of access will come to an abrupt end in the middle of the Great Tribulation when God's bailiff, Michael the archangel and his security squad, throw Satan and his band of rebels out of the courts of Heaven and down to the earth. This event is closer than you think.)

Lucifer, the fallen angel, illustration for the book Paradise Lost, Gustave Dore, 1866.

Now let's get back to our vantage point where we are witnessing the events that are taking place in the Garden of Eden at the moment sin entered the world of man.

Shame, the Bitter Bread of the Sinner Contains the Kernel of Hope!

I want you to see something!

Take a look at Satan's response to the iniquity that entered his heart and compare it with the response of Adam.

Was Satan filled with remorse?

No, he was filled with an elevated pride and hubris.

Satan felt no shame for his lies and exhibited not even a hint of regret or a sliver of self-doubt.

Satan surely expected Adam to find within his heart that same root of bitterness, hatred and resentment.

Look how Adam was being cast out of his home in the Garden of Eden.

Adam would surely join Satan as a new recruit in the army pledged to defile all the works of the Creator.

Surely Adam would be filled with the hot temper of resentment and disdain, and if given the tools would immediately begin to defile the garden, uproot its bountiful fruit trees and vegetation, molest its animal inhabitants and fill the place with shrieks and prideful outbursts against the Most-High.

Surely there would be graffiti in Eden's garden by nightfall, or so thought Satan.

The temptation to sin against the direct command of the Creator had been accomplished masterfully by the serpent.

What happened next must have been a big surprise to Satan.

Adam was not filled with anger and resentment against God.

Adam did not lash out against flora or fauna.

The animals remained unmolested and the garden continued as it had been first created.

This is the first hopeful sign since the disobedient act of rebellion.

Adam was not mad at God but instead was overcome by a crippling sense of sorrow and a desire to find a covering to hide the shocking condition in which he now found himself.

Adam was overcome with SHAME!

Instead of comradery with the fallen creature, Satan found himself temporarily abandoned by them as they nursed the overpowering sense of loss and shame.

God graciously pronounced an edict that stands to this day.

There is to be enmity between the serpent and the women.

The woman Eve, who had heeded the slithering words of the satanically inspired serpent, would have years to ponder all the reasons she should hate and despise the creature that caused her to be deceived and fall into misery.

Satan's desire that the first parents hate and despise God was turned on its head as our first parents now despised the serpent.

If only Adam's seed had rightly regarded the reason for the calamitous condition of mankind and kept kindled both the sorrow for sin and hatred for the one who caused it, what a different world it would be.

Sadly, the lies told to Eve have been repackaged and retold so many times by the Father of Lies that mankind almost immediately came back under the seditious spell of Satan. This time they were ready to rebel properly, according to the Luciferian handbook that spews out hatred and bitter accusations against the Most-High.

Illustration for The Bible panorama, or The Holy Scriptures in picture and story. Author William A. Foster, 1891

Consider two simple facts: one anchored in ancient history and the other a daily occurrence.

Consider that the firstborn of Eve was a murderer, and also consider that almost every time a person dies from some unexpected tragedy, God's goodness is questioned.

God is blamed and His integrity is challenged. He is deemed to be either powerless or secretly malicious.

Good Snake, Bad God?

Every time God is blamed for the results of sin initiated by the evil schemes of Satan, the lie of Satan is advanced.

And what is that lie?

At its very core, it is the following:

God is not really that good.

His words should be heeded with skepticism.

God is keeping mankind from advancing to his full potential.

The Great Irony!

Everything Satan offered Eve she already had waiting for her as the certain consequence of simple obedience motivated by love for her creator.

Consider the irony!

Eve was under the constant care of a loving God who had graciously provided for her every need. God's Words were trustworthy and meant for the welfare of His creatures.

Eve was already on a path that, left uninterrupted by sin, would have resulted in eternal life in a glorified body.

Have we finished our investigation of Adam?

Are we any closer to discovering the clues that will unlock the mystery of how long Adam and Eve were in the garden?

Happily, we have not discovered anything in the biblical narrative that precludes the 33-33.5 years that can be calculated from the vantage point of the Cross of Calvary in 30 AD.

We have finished our inquiry into the meaning of the name of ADAM, examined the possibility that the period of probation in the Garden of Eden might be 40 years.

We have also looked at the biblical account for the birth of Seth occurring when Adam was 130 years old, giving us a period of time that borders Adam and Eve's tenure in the Garden.

The murder of Abel by his brother Cain backdated the birth of Seth by at least 20 years and perhaps more, giving us a time window of no longer than 100-110 years.

Keep in mind that Pattern is Prophecy. Let's see if we can discover the year that Adam sinned in the inkblot patterns revealed about the First Adam and the Last Adam.

CHAPTER 8

33 Years
The Unwitting Witness

Is there Unwitting Eye Witness who is Celebrating the Year Adam Sinned?

Can we add any witnesses to the perspective that Adam and Eve sinned 33 years from Creation?

In this chapter, we will be looking at an unlikely clue. A clue that displays the character, wisdom and longsuffering of the LORD God, YHVH Elohim.

The Unwitting Witness

God has an unrivaled genius for using His enemies to further His own purposes and ends.

You can find this particular pattern repeated over and over again in Scripture.

Wouldn't it be one of the supreme ironies of all time if the LORD God, YHVH Elohim, used the pride and arrogance of Satan to disclose the key missing time-period needed to understand end-times eschatology?

A disclosure meant to encourage the Saints of God to hang on tight to the promises of God, because the end was near.

God displays His wisdom and understanding of all things in what we provincially call the past, present and the future.

Is 33 the Key?

In order to understand the significance of the number 33, you need to ask yourself a few questions.

Have you ever wondered why Lucifer celebrates the number 33?

Have you ever thought about why the number 33 is used with such regularity in the organizations and schemes initiated by Satan?

Why is the number 33 the one premiere number that is advanced and magnified by the Luciferians above all other numbers?

How has Lucifer abused the number 33?

What secret information does it contain that Satan is so proud of yet keeps hidden except to be revealed to his most loyal devotees?

To discover the answer to these questions, you simply need to investigate the Luciferian Sects in order to find out what they are hiding.

Once you have that figured out, you will begin to understand the mystery of the number 33 and how the Luciferians use it to mock and taunt God.

There is no debate about the fact that the number 33 is a code number prominent in all of Lucifer's cults.

Unfortunately, most Christians think the number 33 is taboo.

It is considered an "evil" number that is owned by Lucifer.

Nothing could be further from the truth.

The number 33 is a glorious number that has been hijacked and misused by Lucifer.

Isn't that his specialty?

Lucifer the Infringing Master of the Universe?

Lucifer does nothing original, he simply distorts, abuses, confuses and generally attempts to destroy those things that belong to God.

This is exactly what Lucifer has done with the number 33.

Unfortunately for him, Lucifer is playing checkers while the Creator is playing three-dimensional chess in real-time with one hand behind His back while He is turning every single one of Satan's plans directed at His Children into GOOD.

What Lucifer means for evil, God delights to redeem and return to good.

To discover the mystery surrounding the number 33, let's probe the most prominent Luciferian organization on earth and see if we can discover why they have elevated the number 33.

The Genius of Evil, white marble statue by Guillaume Geefs, 1848.

One organization, which I will not dignify by naming, teaches that once the 33rd degree is reached, the initiated devotee will be illuminated by Lucifer, the Light Bearer.

Does this sound eerily familiar to a conversation recorded in the Scriptures between Eve and the talking Serpent?

Genesis 3:3-7

But of the fruit of the tree which is in the midst of the garden, God hath said, Ye shall not eat of it, neither shall ye touch it, lest ye die.

And the serpent said unto the woman, Ye shall not surely die: For God doth know that in the day ye eat thereof, then

your eyes shall be opened, and ye shall be as gods, knowing good and evil.

Signed Lucifer

And when the woman saw that the tree was good for food, and that it was pleasant to the eyes, and a tree to be desired to make one wise, she took of the fruit thereof, and did eat, and gave also unto her husband with her; and he did eat.

And the eyes of them both were opened, and they knew that they were naked;

Is this why Lucifer is celebrating the number 33?

Is this the answer that has been staring us in the face all the time?

Ask yourself this question:

What is the biggest "achievement" that Lucifer has ever accomplished?

Did Lucifer create an alternate universe more splendid than the one created by YHVH Elohim (the LORD God)?

The answer is NO.

Satan can only corrupt and manipulate God's creative masterpiece.

Satan as a creature is incapable of creating anything original.

Did Satan discover the secret to Eternal Life and pass it along out of the goodness of his heart to all humanity?

The answer is NO!

Satan opened the door to eternal death and all that follow him will discover that Lucifer is a fraud and a liar from the beginning. (Although it must be noted that Satan has simple-minded men who are full of arrogance and pride and decorated with their own letters and degree convinced that they can evolve with the aid of their own technological and biological achievements into the blissful state of the everlasting.)

You must give the devil his due; when he tells a lie it is a whopper.

Satan's Big Achievements!

The only thing that Satan has ever successfully created is confusion, chaos, disinformation, lies, rebellion, death, and destruction.

Satan before the Lord, painting by Corrado Giaquinto, 1750.

These are Satan's big achievements!

Why is Lucifer so excited about the number 33?

Why does he anoint his devotees with the number 33?

The answer is simple and in complete agreement with his prideful and arrogant character.

The answer, I believe, is that the number 33 is connected to the corruption of the pinnacle of Elohim's Creation.

Satan managed through slander, lies and deceit to "illuminate" Adam and Eve on the thirty-third year from Creation.

Satan, the father of lies, managed to put the newly appointed prince of the re-made earth (Adam) on the road to death and destruction.

The sin that removed Adam from his Princely post, as ruler of the earth was the same event that elevated Lucifer to his current position, as the god of this world, the prince of the power of the air. His current status and position is a result of Adam's fall from grace.

I do not pretend to understand the Celestial statutes that regulate this transfer of authority from fallen man to a fallen angel. I only know it happened according to the decrees of Heaven which are perfect, but often hard to understand.

How might Satan celebrate his ill-gotten devilish victory in his strategic war against the Most High?

The Fall of Man (detail), painting by Cornelis van Haarlem, 1592.

2 Corinthians 11:3, 14

But I fear, lest by any means, as the serpent beguiled Eve through his subtlety, so your minds should be corrupted from the simplicity that is in Christ.

And no marvel; for Satan himself is transformed into an angel of light.

Is the number 33 important to Satan because it is the number that marks the year that he became the prince of the earth, the prince of this world, the very year after God's Creation that he "illuminated" Eve?

I am proposing that this is exactly what happened.

In fairness to the reader, I must couch my enthusiasm for this theory with the word "possibly."

Satan Exulting over Eve (detail), watercolor by William Blake, 1795.

I humbly offer this suggestion for your consideration.

We MAY be getting closer to confirming the prophetic witness in the Berisheet End-Times Passover Prophecy

Have we discovered the answer to the question that has puzzled Bible scholars for thousands of years?

How long was Adam in the Garden of Eden?

The Unwitting Witness

The first unwitting witness may give us the exact time-stamp confirmation that answers the question regarding Adam and Eve's tenure in the Garden of Eden before they were evicted.

This time-stamp may have been unwittingly given to us by Lucifer himself.

Satan's exuberant and prideful display of the year he "illuminated" our first parent may be a witness to the year that the Dispensation of Innocence jarringly and sadly came to a conclusion.

We propose that the year just might be 33-33.5 Anno Mundi, after Creation!

CHAPTER 9

30 AD
The Last Adam Succeeds!

Pattern is Prophecy
Numeric clue discovered in the Two Adams.

We are told in Scripture that there are two Adams.

The Scriptures declare the sinful works of the first Adam and the righteous works of the Last Adam.

We begin this chapter by reminding the reader that we are still gathering clues that will answer the question, *How long was Adam in the Garden of Eden before he sinned?*

Are there any clues that would tell us how long Adam was in the Garden of Eden hidden in the name of Adam, revealed in the Pictures and Numbers of his name?

Let's begin by looking at the Picture that God has provided us of the First Adam.

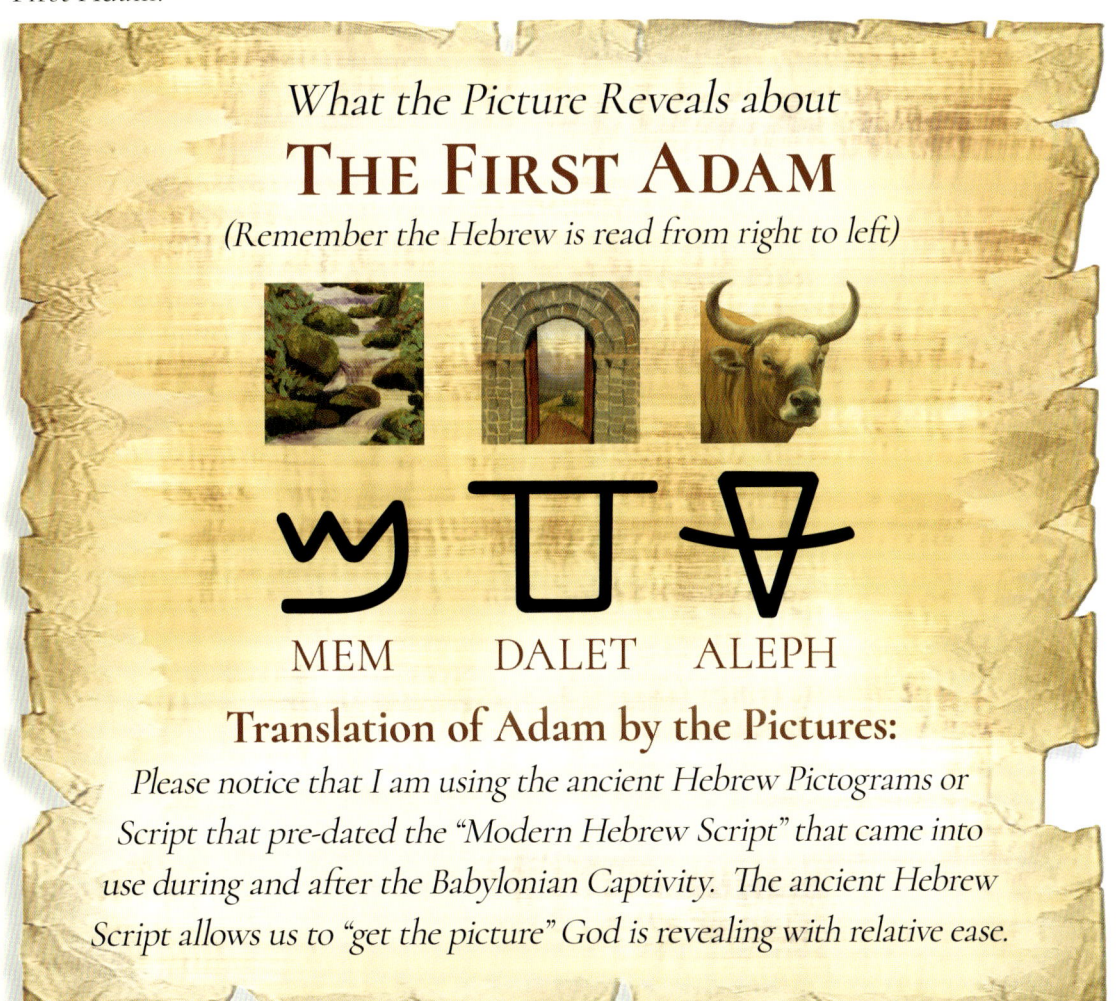

What the Picture Reveals about
THE FIRST ADAM
(Remember the Hebrew is read from right to left)

MEM   DALET   ALEPH

Translation of Adam by the Pictures:
Please notice that I am using the ancient Hebrew Pictograms or Script that pre-dated the "Modern Hebrew Script" that came into use during and after the Babylonian Captivity. The ancient Hebrew Script allows us to "get the picture" God is revealing with relative ease.

THE BERISHEET END-TIMES PASSOVER PROPHECY
CHAPTER 9: 30 AD, THE LAST ADAM SUCCEEDS!

The pictographic translation is simple.

Adam was the first man ▽ and representative leader who opened the Door ⊓ that led to the pathway that ended in chaos, confusion and death ᗰ.

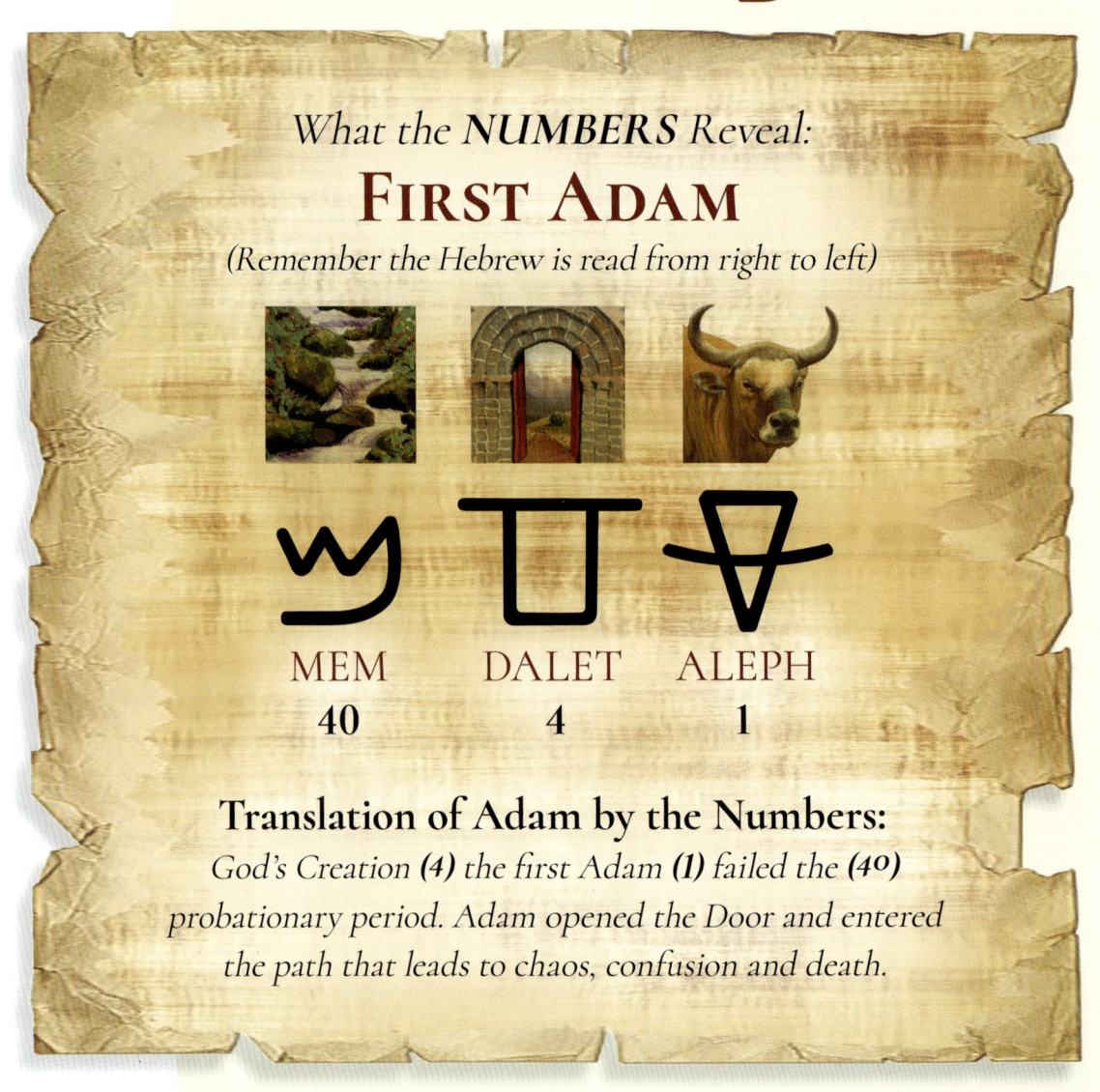

What the NUMBERS Reveal:
First Adam
(Remember the Hebrew is read from right to left)

MEM	DALET	ALEPH
40	4	1

Translation of Adam by the Numbers:
God's Creation **(4)** the first Adam **(1)** failed the **(40)** probationary period. Adam opened the Door and entered the path that leads to chaos, confusion and death.

The First Adam was cast out of the Garden of Eden and into a world that would remind him of the consequences of his rebellion against the Lord who created and loved him.

Adam was cast out, but not forsaken, by His Creator who graciously promised to send a Messiah who would atone for the sins of Adam and his children, including you and me.

God showed favor to both Adam and his seed by providing Himself as the Door that leads to Eternal Life. There is hope of revival and restoration through the finished work of Yeshua Ha-Mashiach, the Last Adam.

What the NUMBERS Reveal: FIRST ADAM

(Remember the Hebrew is read from right to left)

MEM   DALET   ALEPH

We have already explored the mystery of the Hebrew letter Mem. It is a Hebrew letter that can have a double and opposite meaning. Mem can mean Chaos and Death caused by a flood or tsunami or it can be the picture of Water and Life.

The Apostle Paul summarized succinctly this difference in his letter to the gathering of first-century believers living in the city of Corinth.

> **1 CORINTHIANS 15:22**
>
> *For as in Adam all die, so in Christ all will be made alive.*

We could easily end the mystery of the Last Adam on this high and hopeful note. But there is another mystery we must unravel in order to fully understand the significance of the last Adam.

> **2 CORINTHIANS 5:21**
>
> *For our sake he made him to be **sin** who **knew no sin**, so that in him we might become the righteousness of God.*

Biblical Patterns are Prophecy!

One of the secrets to understanding the images dramatized in the living words of Scripture can be found in the Biblical Prophetic Patterns.

In other words, the scenes that are shaped by the words of Scripture are meant to establish in our minds and imagination a pattern that is very often prophetic. This vantage point is largely unfamiliar to the western mindset.

We can connect the dots when we are clearly told that "such and such happens" and then "such and such will occur."

We do not do as well with shadows and types. Unfortunately, without this added perspective provided by pictures and numbers, we often miss the prophetic patterns that dominate the storylines of the ancient prophetic Scriptures.

The Eastern mind "gets the picture" with relative ease while the Western mind struggles to free itself from the shackles of the Greek and Roman philosophical systems of thought and the anti-supernatural bias and humanism that has swept the modern world in the name of science and technology.

Now let's return to the question we are investigating.

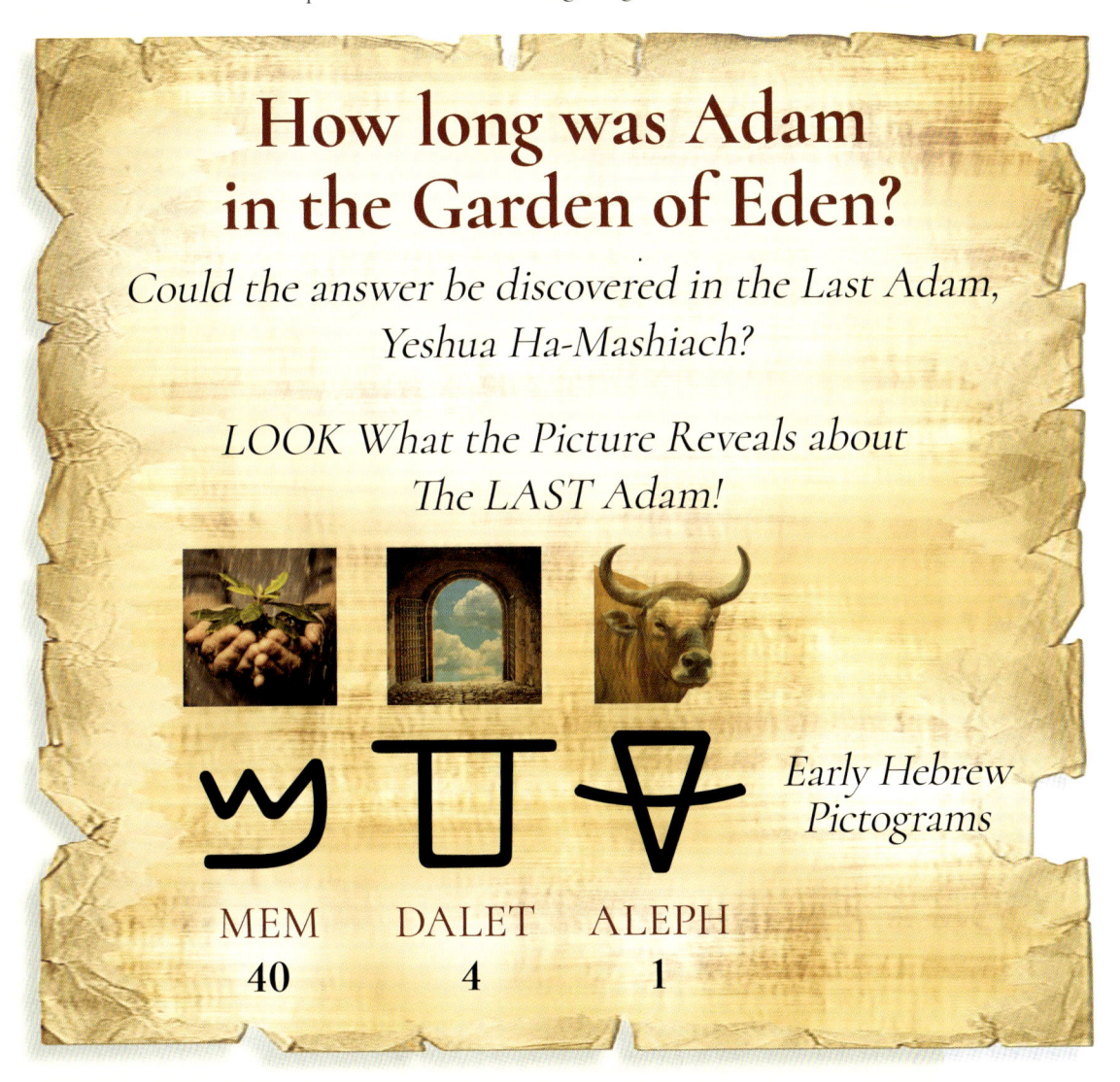

How long was Adam in the Garden of Eden?

Could the answer be discovered in the Last Adam, Yeshua Ha-Mashiach?

LOOK What the Picture Reveals about The LAST Adam!

Early Hebrew Pictograms

MEM	DALET	ALEPH
40	4	1

Let us go back to the "Ichabod" moment in the Garden of Eden.

The clinched jaw of Adam released the curse and the glory literally departs.

Adam can be seen standing in front of a tree naked and full of sin, despised and about to be rejected.

Fast forward to the scene taking place in another garden.

View the Last Adam hanging naked upon a tree having become sin, despised and rejected.

> ## ROMANS 5:14
> *Nevertheless, death reigned from Adam to Moses, even over them that had not sinned after the similitude of Adam's transgression, who is the figure of him that was to come.*

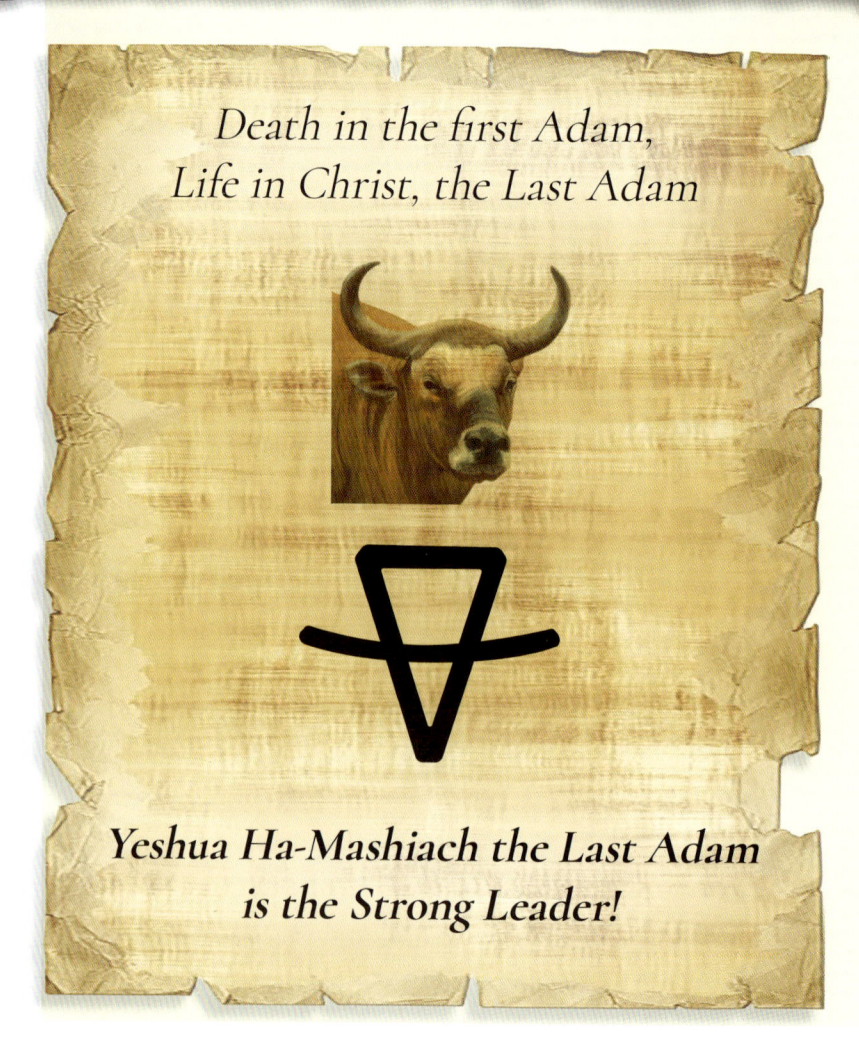

*Death in the first Adam,
Life in Christ, the Last Adam*

**Yeshua Ha-Mashiach the Last Adam
is the Strong Leader!**

Psalm 25:5

Lead me in thy truth and teach me: for thou art the God of my salvation; on thee do I wait all the day.

Revelation 7:17

For the Lamb which is in the midst of the throne shall feed them, and shall **lead** them unto living fountains of waters: and God shall wipe away all tears from their eyes.

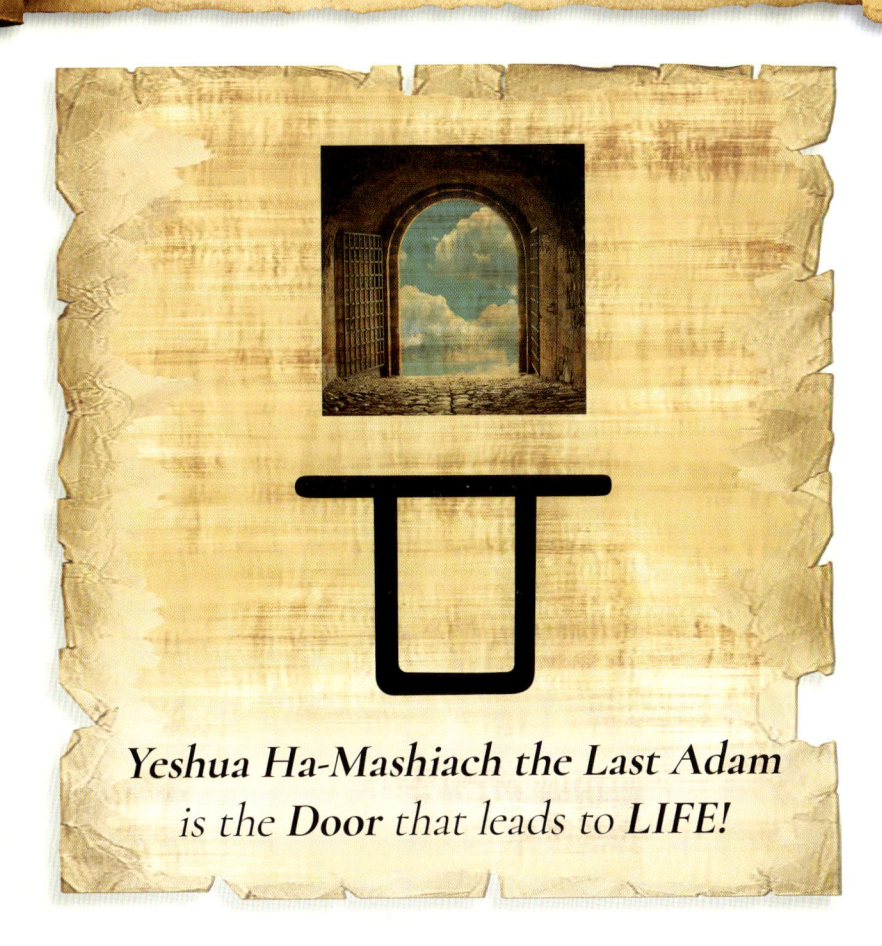

Yeshua Ha-Mashiach the Last Adam is the Door that leads to LIFE!

Matthew 7:13-14

*Enter ye in at the **strait gate**: for wide is the gate, and broad is the way, that leadeth to destruction, and many there be which go in thereat: Because strait is the gate, and narrow is the way, which leadeth unto life, and few there be that find it.*

John 10:9

*I am the **door**: by me if any man enter in, he shall be saved, and shall go in and out, and find pasture.*

Yeshua Ha-Mashiach the Last Adam is the Living Water!

Psalm 63:1

*O God, thou art my God; early will I seek thee: my soul thirsteth for thee, my flesh longeth for thee in a dry and **thirsty** land, where no water is.*

John 4:14

*But whosoever drinketh of the **water** that I shall give him shall never thirst; but the **water** that I shall give him shall be in him a well of **water** springing up into everlasting life.*

John 4:10

*Jesus answered and said unto her, If thou knewest the gift of God, and who it is that saith to thee, Give me to drink; thou wouldest have asked of him, and he would have given thee **living water.***

Revelation 21:6

*And he said unto me, It is done. I am Alpha and Omega, the beginning and the end. I will give unto him that is athirst of the fountain of the **water** of life freely.*

Where the First Adam failed, the Last Adam, Jesus the Christ succeeded.

Permit me to share an insight that will bring the majesty of the Last Adam's mission into sharp focus.

Aleph, as we learned, is the Strong Leader, The First.

And when we put Dalet and Mem, the 2nd and 3rd letters of Adam's name together we get the picture of the Pathway of the Waters or Liquid.

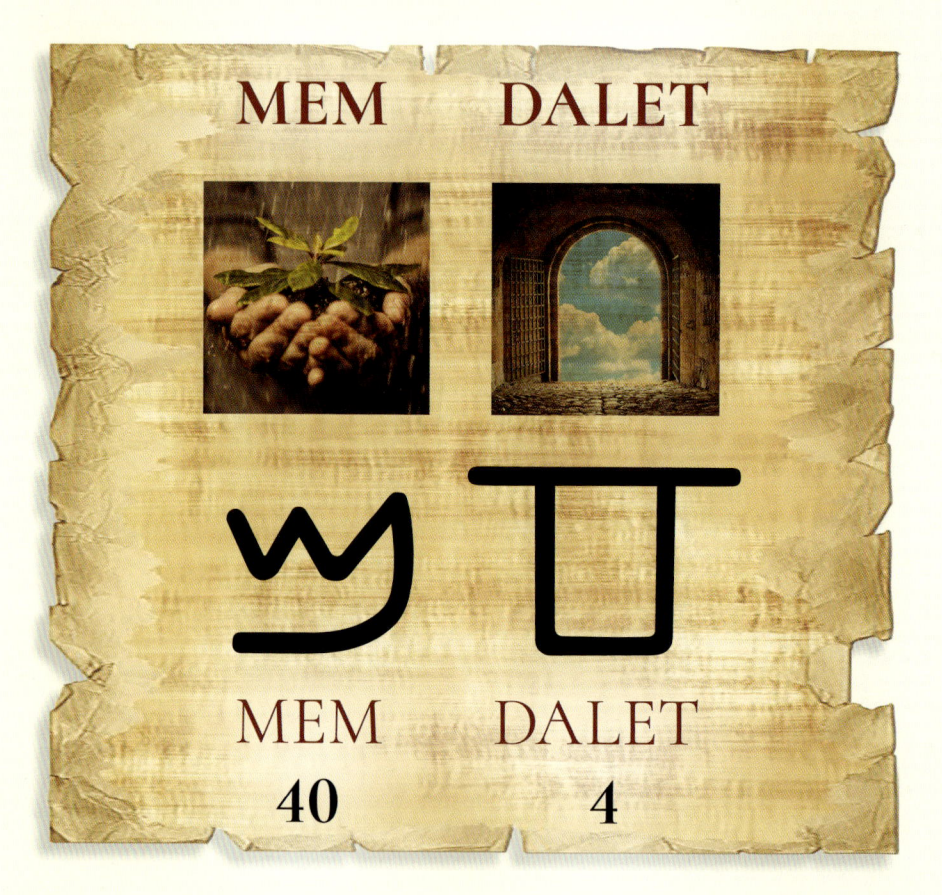

MEM   **DALET**

MEM   **DALET**
40   **4**

And what word do the letters Dalet and Mem compose in Conventional Hebrew?

The answer is BLOOD.

The Pathway of the Liquid.

Everyone, man, woman and child who ever lived or ever will live, is **Under the Blood of the Strong Leader!**

The only question is this:

Which Strong Leader's BLOOD Are YOU Under?

MEM	DALET	MEM	DALET
40	4	40	4

The Scriptures reveal that Yeshua Ha-Mashiach has come to shed His precious blood as an atonement for sin for all those that repent, call upon His name and receive Him alone as their Savior.

THE BERISHEET END-TIMES PASSOVER PROPHECY
CHAPTER 9: 30 AD, THE LAST ADAM SUCCEEDS!

Once you receive Messiah you are under the blood of Yeshua Ha-Mashiach, Jesus the Christ. The blood of Jesus that covers your sins results in the forgiveness that can be granted by no other means.

You were born by default under the blood of the first Adam.

Without Christ, you are under the same curse as Adam and the end result of that curse, unless God intervenes, is death and hell. Man has Adam's mark, the Y chromosome, in their very DNA.

Mankind is under the curse and without Divine intervention can only look forward to the God's wrath and eternal separation from our Lord and Creator.

In 1 Corinthians 15:45 we read these words:

1 Corinthians 15:45

And so it is written, **The first man Adam** *was made a living soul; the* **last Adam** *was made a quickening spirit.*

Jesus our Lord is called the Last Adam.

The Last Adam came to earth to open up another door so that we might travel down another path.

A path that leads to eternal life.

John 14:6

Jesus saith unto him, I am the way, the truth, and the life: no man cometh unto the Father, but by me.

Yeshua is the only door, the only path that leads to eternal life. Jesus is the only door to Heaven which He has prepared for those He redeemed by His blood sacrifice on the Cross of Calvary.

All other paths lead to death and destruction.

Now you know the mystery hidden in the name of Adam.

Yeshua Ha-Mashiach instructed those that relied on the Ancient Prophetic Text to save them to look again with a solemn concern and fear for the condition and final destination of their soul.

Yeshua told them that they had missed the one thing, the only thing upon which they could build a foundation of hope.

What was it they had missed?

They had missed Him.

Was He hidden?

The answer that Yeshua gave was instructive.

They were blind and could not see what was right in front of them.

The Scriptures were speaking and disclosing throughout all its letters or Script, through all its words and sentences and paragraphs. Always disclosing one singular and overarching truth. The truth was staring them in the face all along.

Who was it that was in their presence, hidden from blind unbelieving eyes and hard hearts?

It was Yeshua Ha-Mashiach.

And what does He instruct us to do?

He tells us to search, investigate as if you're looking for hidden treasure! And what are we to thoroughly search and investigate? The answer is the Scriptures.

What is the prize that will be found?

It is Yeshua the Savior, the one who stands ready to give to all that call upon His name in repentance and faith the gift of eternal life.

The First Failure

The sanctuary of the Garden of Eden has become off-limits to Adam, his wife Eve and all his offspring.

Is there no hope for Adam and his offspring?

The answer to that question is found in the one thing that left the Garden of Eden, along with Adam and Eve, unmolested by sin.

And what was that one thing?

The gift of the pure, uncorrupted language of the Garden is the one precious gift left for Adam and Eve.

The precious pure language used to reveal the Last Adam.

The Berisheet End-Times Passover Prophecy informs us that there are...

4000 YEARS

between the Sin of Rebellion by the FIRST Adam in **3970 BC** and the Sin Atonement of the Last Adam Accomplished in **30 AD**

CHAPTER 10

Pattern is Prophecy

The groundwork has been put in place and now we are ready to discover the first solid clue as to the number of years that Adam lived in the Garden of Eden.

We will leave the most convincing clues for the end.

We will begin with the clues that might better be called "hints."

By themselves, they may seem unconvincing, but when you start putting them all together a pattern and picture emerges that is both authoritative and difficult to refute.

Pattern is Prophecy

In light of this biblical interpretive principle, I would like you to consider the following parallels between the First and the Last Adam.

THE FIRST ADAM | THE LAST ADAM

THE FIRST ADAM	THE LAST ADAM
The First Adam was miraculously created and is called a son of God.	**The Last Adam** was miraculously born of a virgin and identified Himself as "the son of Man" (Son of Adam). **The Last Adam** was Immanuel, the un-created only Begotten Son of God.
The First Adam had unbroken fellowship with God the Father until the day that he fell into sin while in the Garden of Eden.	**The Last Adam** had unbroken fellowship with God the Father until He took upon Himself the sins of man as cruel hands lifted Him up in a garden.
The moment **The First Adam** sinned, he forsook his relationship with the Heavenly Father.	The moment **The Last Adam** took upon Himself the sins of the world, He was momentarily forsaken by His Heavenly Father.

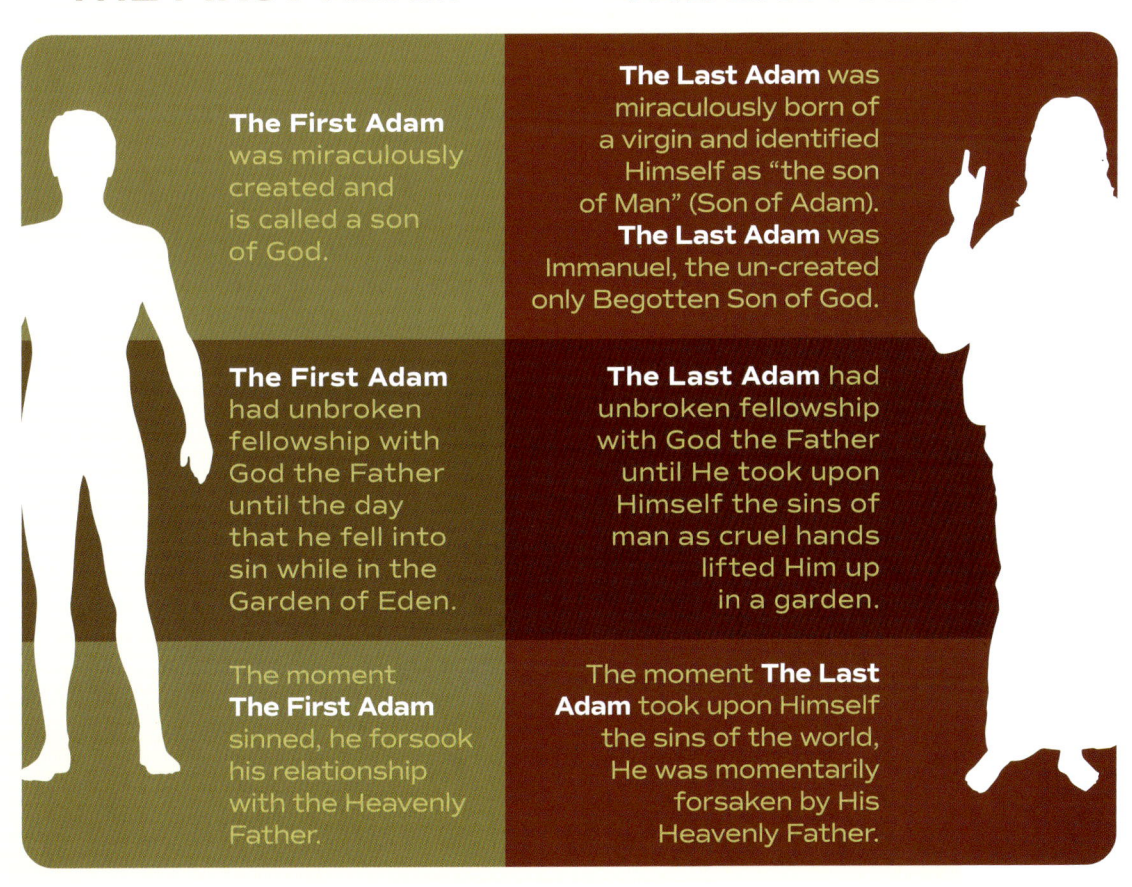

THE FIRST ADAM	THE LAST ADAM
The First Adam was not deceived by the Serpent and willingly disobeyed his Heavenly Father. (It is presumed to this day that he sinned in order to preserve his relationship with his wife Eve. While sinful man might consider this a noble act of self-sacrifice, it was actually an act of treachery and rebellion against his loving Heavenly Father.)	**The Last Adam** was not deceived by the Serpent and willingly obeyed His Heavenly Father as He took on the sins of mankind in order to provide a way to restore the relationship between sinful man and the Heavenly Father.
The First Adam stood naked and ashamed before the Tree of the Knowledge of Good and Evil.	**The Last Adam** was stripped naked, "stood up" and nailed to a dead tree.
Eve stretched out her arm and grasped the forbidden fruit.	**The Last Adam** obediently stretched His arms out and grasped the iron nail.
The First Adam made the journey from sinless to sinful and was cursed in a split second of time.	**The Last Adam** made the journey from sinless to a cursed sinner in a split second of time, as He became sin for us.
The First Adam entered into a covenant of death when he breached the conditional covenant of life by his disobedience.	**The Last Adam** nullified the covenant of death and reinitiated the covenant of life by His obedience.
Eve stood upon the ground and looked up at the delicious fruit hanging overhead and desired it.	**The Last Adam** was hung up on a dead tree and looked down at the sinners standing on the ground and desired them.
The drama in which **The First Adam** was the focus, took place in a garden.	The drama in which **The Last Adam** was the focus, took place in a garden.

THE FIRST ADAM	THE LAST ADAM
The moment **The First Adam** ate the forbidden fruit, he died spiritually and began to decay physically, a process that resulted in his death.	Hours after **The Last Adam** heaped upon Himself the sins of the world, He died physically.
The First Adam immediately experienced the overwhelming sense of shame after disobeying God and tried to cover his shame with leaves.	**The Last Adam** after heaping upon Himself the sins of the world, experienced an overwhelming sense of separation from His Heavenly Father so that sinners might cover their shame with His own blood.
The First Adam physically died outside a garden.	**The Last Adam** died and was laid in a tomb inside a garden.
The First Adam died, his body decayed, and he returned to the dust of the earth.	**The Last Adam** died. His body did not decay. He rose from the dead after three days and nights and returned to His place in Heaven.
The First Adam lost the God-granted authority over the earth when he sinned. His authority was given to Satan who became the god of this world.	**The Last Adam** took back the legal authority over the kingdoms of the world that was lost by the first Adam.
God announced to the woman, **Eve,** that through her seed the promised Messiah would come in order to roll back the curse of sin.	**The Last Adam** after His resurrection from the dead, announced Himself to a woman and told her not to touch Him because He had not yet returned to the father in order to present the blood sacrifice that reversed the curse of sin.

THE FIRST ADAM	THE LAST ADAM
The First Adam left Paradise in disgrace.	The Last Adam returned to Paradise proclaiming grace.
The First Adam left Paradise with a friend.	The Last Adam entered Paradise with a friend.
The First Adam lived in a perfect world with no sin where he disobeyed the one simple commandment given to him by his Heavenly Father.	The Last Adam lived in a corrupt sinful world where He obeyed all the commandments of His Heavenly Father perfectly. The Last Adam accomplished the one amazingly difficult thing His Heavenly Father asked Him to do. He took the cup of suffering and death so that we might live.
The First Adam opened the door to chaos, confusion and death	The Last Adam opened the door to eternal life.
The First Adam returned to the dust.	The Last Adam returned to Heaven.
The First Adam loved his bride more than anything else.	The Last Adam loved His Heavenly Father more than anything else.

The Last Adam

took upon Himself the sins of the world as He was nailed to a wooden tree where He physically died at the age of…

Thirty-Three and a half years old.

How old do you imagine **The First Adam** was when he spiritually died?

Pattern Really is Prophecy!

Could it be that thirty-three years after His miraculous Creation Adam stood naked before the Tree of the Knowledge of Good and Evil where he willingly disobeyed his Heavenly Father?

A New Beginning

The Time-Stamp prophecy that YHVH Elohim embedded into the first word of the Scriptures did not begin at the moment of Creation but 33-33.5 years after Creation. The time-stamp is identifying the year that Adam sinned.

We have two prophetic fulfillments—one predicted with clarity, the other can be easily deduced. Both are 4000 years.

Only God could make this happen with such precision.

This means that the first Adam was born on 1 Anno Mundi, in the first year of Creation.

This also means that the "Last Adam" was born in the year 4 BC, which just happens to be the one date that is not only the agreed upon but the only one that does not create time-span paradoxes at both ends.

The first Adam took his firsts steps in the garden of Eden on 1 Anno Mundi

God prophetically reveals from day one, even before sin entered the world, that deliverance would be needed and would arrive on schedule exactly 4000 years from the very day and year that the first Adam sinned, exactly 33-33.5 years after His Creation.

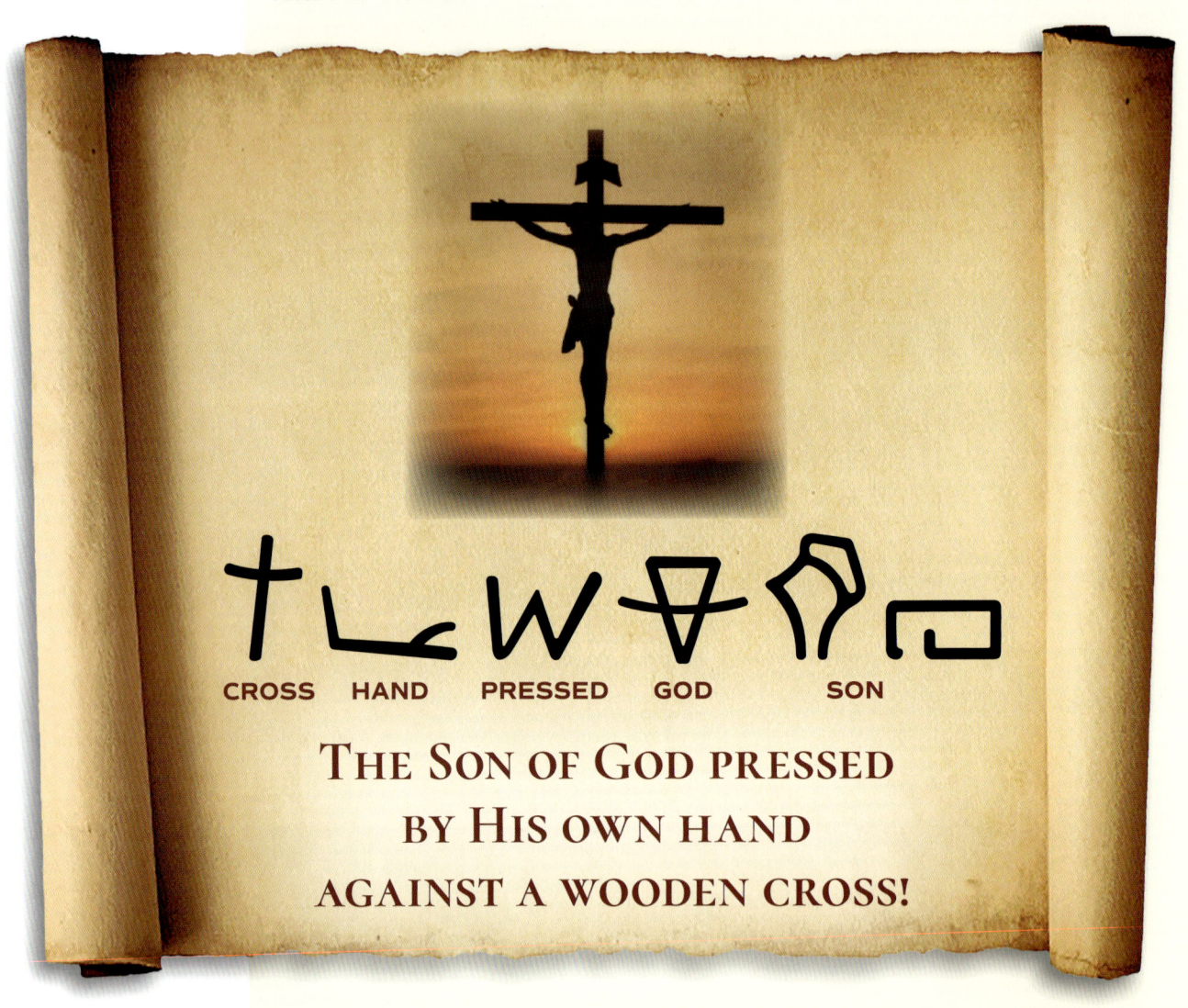

CROSS HAND PRESSED GOD SON

The Son of God pressed by His own hand against a wooden cross!

The Berisheet Prophecy clearly reveals the Greatest Beginning of All Time. The Beginning that ends man's covenant with sin and death. The Beginning that makes a way where there was no way.

The way that has been opened up for us by the only begotten Son of God. This Son of God is the Prince of Glory who left His Home in Heaven to Come to earth as a servant in order to Joyfully accomplish His Heavenly Father's plan and purpose to redeem fallen mankind.

CHAPTER 11

The End!

The Great Day of His Wrath, painting by John Martin, 1851.

Why God guides and directs His children is not a mystery.

He simply loves us and wants us to stay safe and sound!

If we seek His leadership, the prerequisite conditions are spelled out clearly in His word.

> ## Proverbs 3:5-6
> *Trust in the Lord with all thine heart; and lean not unto thine own understanding. In all thy ways acknowledge him, and he shall direct thy paths.*

The promise is that if we trust Him, do not rely on our own understanding and subordinate to His perfect understanding, acknowledge Him in all our ways, that He will direct our paths.

Is there anyone who doesn't think it would be amazing for God to take an interest in directing our humble paths as we make our pilgrimage through this hazardous and dangerous world, a world that has been corrupted by sin and is in bondage to the Prince of Darkness, who desires more than anything to destroy us?

Are you uncertain about where you're going to end up?

The solution is simple.

Let God direct your path!

How God directs His children in His paths is often a mystery.

The methods God uses to direct His children are as different as His children.

Some require a vision or a dream to get them started, others find clear paths with the aid of the Holy Spirit as they read the Scriptures with childlike faith!

Why Now?

Obviously, the disclosure in this book, if accepted as viable, puts us on the cusp of the final moments in history.

I am watching the sweeping second hand, knowing in my spirit and by all the evidence at hand including the Berisheet End-Times Passover Prophecy hidden in the first word of the Bible, that we are in the last seconds before the glorification of the body of Christ.

Is there a grander expectation?

Is that the answer to why this is being revealed at this late hour?

Is it the lateness of the hour that has beckoned this mystery to manifest. Why else would a mystery so splendid and clear be hidden since the time that Moses first scribed the Torah, letter by letter?

Was it missed out of carelessness?

No.

Was it missed in order to accomplish a specific purpose?

That is the only answer that resonates with my spirit.

Imagine, hidden in the beginning reserved for a full disclosure at the very end.

Why me?

Why was I given the privilege of finding this hidden key?

If you're looking for an answer I would point you to the only one that makes any sense to me.

> ## 2 KINGS 7:8-9
>
> *8 And when these lepers came to the uttermost part of the camp, they went into one tent, and did eat and drink, and carried thence silver, and gold, and raiment, and went and hid it; and came again, and entered into another tent, and carried thence also, and went and hid it.*
>
> *9 Then they said one to another, We do not well: this day is a day of good tidings, and we hold our peace: if we tarry till the morning light, some mischief will come upon us: now therefore come, that we may go and tell the king's household.*

The following is a simple, honest confession from a child of God who would never be surprised if he was wrong. A child that is miffed that he seems to be holding the most amazing prophetic puzzle piece to be disclosed in recent memory.

The Four IF'S

If the Sabbath Millennial Prophetic Perspective is correct and I believe it is!

If the Pre-Millennial Prophetic Perspective is correct and I believe it with all my heart!

If our calendar is correct from 30 AD until today, and I have no reason to believe it isn't.

If the three time-stamp Prophecies discovered in the "Beginning" Berisheet End-Times Passover Prophecy revealed in Genesis 1:1 is the 1st Prophecy in the Bible...

Then this is a calendar of what happened and when it happened in the Past.

4004 BC

6 days of Creation, 7th day of Rest

Genesis 2:1-4

Thus the Heavens and the earth were finished, and all the host of them.

And on the seventh day God ended his work which he had made; and he rested on the seventh day from all his work which he had made.

And God blessed the seventh day, and sanctified it: because that in it he had rested from all his work which God created and made.

These are the generations of the Heavens and of the earth when they were created, in the day that the Lord God made the earth and the Heavens,

3970 BC
Adam sinned at the age of 33-33.5

Adam is cast out of the Garden of Eden

The Age of Innocence ending abruptly with the Sin of Adam.

Genesis 2:1-4

And when the woman saw that the tree was good for food, and that it was pleasant to the eyes, and a tree to be desired to make one wise, she took of the fruit thereof, and did eat, and gave also unto her husband with her; and he did eat.

And the eyes of them both were opened, and they knew that they were naked; and they sewed fig leaves together, and made themselves aprons.

And they heard the voice of the Lord God walking in the garden in the cool of the day: and Adam and his wife hid themselves from the presence of the Lord God amongst the trees of the garden.

And the Lord God called unto Adam, and said unto him, Where art thou?

And he said, I heard thy voice in the garden, and I was afraid, because I was naked; and I hid myself.

4 BC

Miraculous Birth of Immanuel – Messiah
(exactly 4000 years from Creation

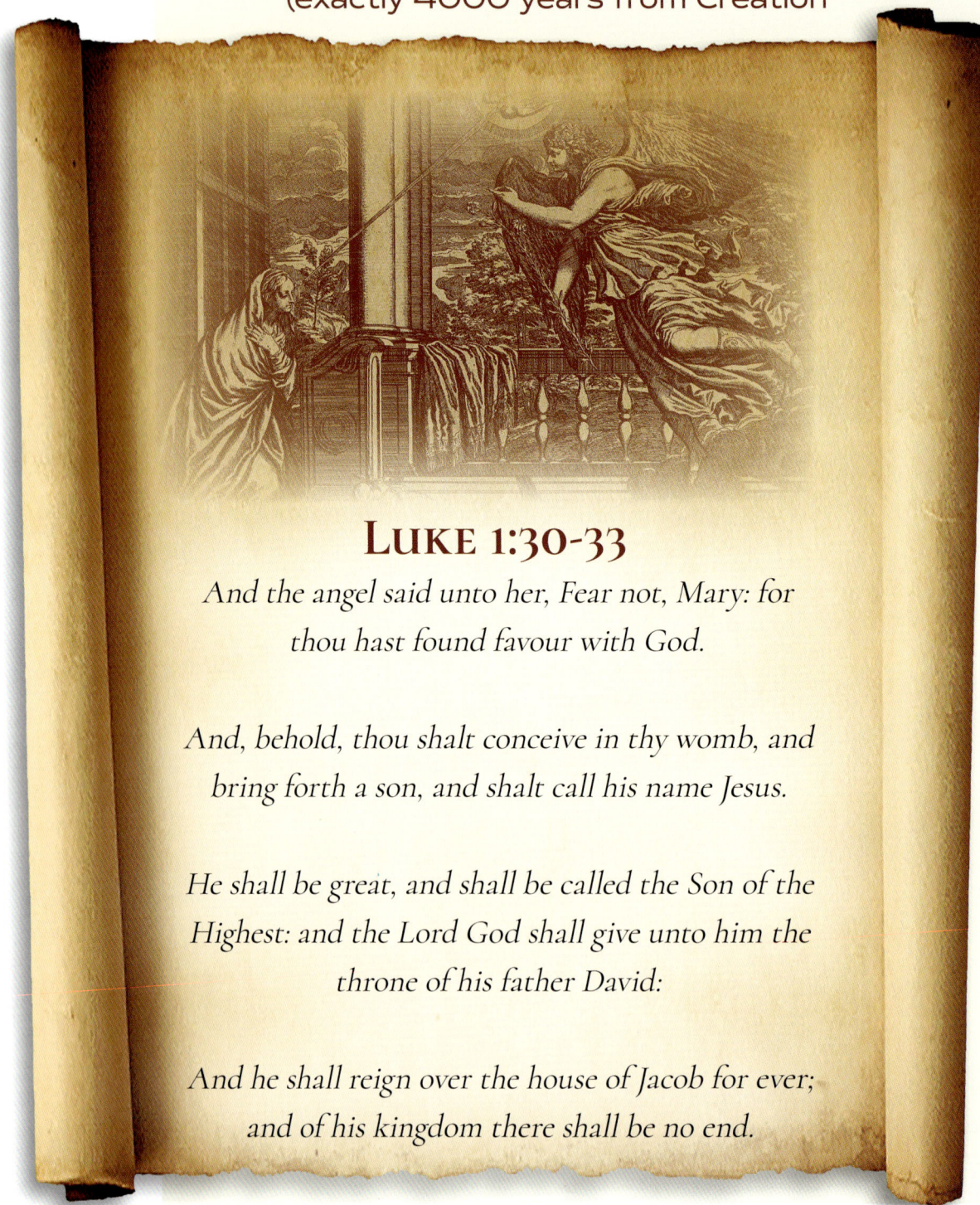

Luke 1:30-33

And the angel said unto her, Fear not, Mary: for thou hast found favour with God.

And, behold, thou shalt conceive in thy womb, and bring forth a son, and shalt call his name Jesus.

He shall be great, and shall be called the Son of the Highest: and the Lord God shall give unto him the throne of his father David:

And he shall reign over the house of Jacob for ever; and of his kingdom there shall be no end.

30 AD

Christch Dies on the Cross of Calvary

John 19:16-19

Then delivered he him therefore unto them to be crucified. And they took Jesus, and led him away.

And he bearing his cross went forth into a place called the place of a skull, which is called in the Hebrew Golgotha:

Where they crucified him, and two other with him, on either side one, and Jesus in the midst.

And Pilate wrote a title, and put it on the cross. And the writing was Jesus Of Nazareth The King Of The Jews.

30 AD - 1948

Church Age and the Super Sign that identifies the Terminal Generation.

> **JEREMIAH 30:2,3**
>
> *Thus speaketh the Lord God of Israel, saying, Write thee all the words that I have spoken unto thee in a book.*
>
> *For, lo, the days come, saith the Lord, that I will bring again the captivity of my people Israel and Judah, saith the Lord: and I will cause them to return to the land that I gave to their fathers, and they shall possess it.*

Using the millennial yardstick provided in the Berisheet End-Times Passover Prophecy we have laid a line that took us back in time to the year that Adam sinned.

From those two reference points, we have discovered two prophetic dates that point us to the past where we find laying seamlessly on both sides of this prophetic time stamp, two more major prophetic events.

We have discovered the year the first Adam was created in 4004 BC.

We have discovered the year Adam sinned in 3970 BC.

We have discovered the year Jesus the Christ was born in 4 BC.

All from the vantage point of the Crucifixion of Christ in 30 AD.

If you believe that these dates prove the failure of the Genesis 1 prophecy, as they are at odds by thousand if not millions of years with the world's timeline for the genesis of mankind, then this prophetic perspective is not for you.

If on the other hand you believe that these dates are both biblical and believable then the additional prophetic harbingers embedded in the Berisheet End-Times Passover Prophecy should be taken very seriously in light of the accuracy of this prophecy as it has unfolded precisely in the past based on God's Word.

Notice what will happen in the Future based on the Berisheet End-Times Passover Prophecy

Church Age
30 AD....?
But no later than 2023 AD

Sometime between the publication of this book in 2018 and 2023, based on the Millennial time-stamps that appear to be revealed in the Berisheet End-Times Passover Prophecy, the collective Church of Christ is to be taken up in the blink of an eye to meet our Savior in the air.

> ### 1 Thessalonians 4:16-18
> *For the Lord himself shall descend from Heaven with a shout, with the voice of the archangel, and with the trump of God: and the dead in Christ shall rise first:*
>
> *Then we which are alive and remain shall be caught up together with them in the clouds, to meet the Lord in the air: and so shall we ever be with the Lord.*
>
> *Wherefore comfort one another with these words.*

The Church Age comes to a conclusion with the Departure of the Church that is called up to be with the Lord in the air.

Please take notice that the Departure of the Church happens before the Great Tribulation also known as the "Time of Jacob's Trouble" and "the 70th Week of Daniel."

To be clear, the Departure of the Church precedes the Great Tribulation but it does not trigger the Great Tribulation.

The Departure of the Church happens before the 70th Week of Daniel but also independently of the 70th Week of Daniel.

What does this mean?

It means that it is not unreasonable and very likely that there could be many months, if not years, between the Rapture of the Church and the start-date for the Great Tribulation, the 70th Week of Daniel.

Just to be crystal clear, the "Departure of the Church," often referred to as the Rapture according to the Berisheet time-line, takes place sometime between the publication of this book in (2018 AD – 2023 AD) *But it DOES NOT trigger* the start of the Great Tribulation or The 70th Week of Daniel.

This period of Tribulation will last for 1 week of years that are 360 days in length, or **7 years** less 37 days, according to the book of Daniel.

The Great Tribulation **IS NOT** connected by a time sequence with the Rapture of the Church.

The Great Tribulation **IS** connected by a time sequence with the Second Coming of Christ. The Second Coming will immediately follow on the heels of the Great Tribulation.

If you're a member of the body of Christ, then you will not be on earth to witness the Great Tribulation or the Second Coming of Christ.

Notice I did not say that the departed church **would not** witness the Second Coming, **just not** from the vantage point as one who is dwelling on the earth.

1 Thessalonians 4:16-18

13 To the end he may stablish your hearts unblameable in holiness before God, even our Father, at the coming of our Lord Jesus Christ with all his saints.

Jude 14

14 And Enoch also, the seventh from Adam, prophesied of these, saying, Behold, the Lord cometh with ten thousands of his saints,

Revelation 19:14

14 And the armies which were in Heaven followed him upon white horses, clothed in fine linen, white and clean.

2023 AD

The Second Coming of Christ, based on the Berisheet End-Times Passover Prophecy, will happen in the year 2030 AD on God's Millennial Calendar exactly 2000 years from the Cross of Calvary and **after 2000 years** from His first arrival in 4 BC as promised by the prophet Hosea.

> ## Hosea 6:1-3
>
> *Come, and let us return unto the Lord: for he hath torn, and he will heal us; he hath smitten, and he will bind us up.*
>
> *After two days will he revive us: in the third day he will raise us up, and we shall live in his sight.*
>
> *Then shall we know, if we follow on to know the Lord: his going forth is prepared as the morning; and he shall come unto us as the rain, as the latter and former rain unto the earth.*

Please note that Christ comes after two days and raises Israel up on the third day.

To keep this simple, notice that the 2030 Berisheet Prophecy fulfills the prophecy of Hosea.

There are 2033 years between 4 BC and 2030 AD.

The Second Day was fulfilled between 4 BC and 1996 (exactly 2000 years – or 2 millennial days).

According to the Berisheet End-Times Passover Prophecy, the Hosea prophecy regarding the Third Day could begin just one minute after the 2000 years between 30 AD (Calvary) and 2030 AD (the start date for the Millennial Kingdom of Christ).

Keep in mind that the Third Day on God's Millennial Calendar has a beginning and an end. It begins in 2030 AD and ends in 3030 AD, a period of 1000 years.

The Second Coming of Christ is easy to date once the Great Tribulation begins since the signs and time periods that are included in this period are clearly revealed in the Scripture.

3030 AD - ETERNITY
(Forever and Ever time without end...)

Destruction of Earth by fire followed by a new Heaven and a new Earth and the eternal state.

> ### 2 Peter 3:7
> *But the Heavens and the earth, which are now, by the same word are kept in store, reserved unto fire against the day of judgment and perdition of ungodly men.*
>
> ### 2 Peter 3:12
> *Looking for and hasting unto the coming of the day of God, wherein the Heavens being on fire shall be dissolved, and the elements shall melt with fervent heat?*

All these time forecasts are based on the fulfillment of the 4000-year prophecy found in the first word in the Scriptures and the actual unfolding of events in history. Remember that the prophetic timelines in this book are not based on the start point of Creation but the start date of the crucifixion of Christ.

We propose that this date is 30 AD. Many others disagree. We respect other opinions and would simply point out that the Berisheet Passover Prophecy does not depend on the 30 AD date and the substitution of any other date simply shifts the timelines that all have their beginning at the date of the cross.

The Berisheet End-Times Passover Prophecy does not forecast the year of Creation, except as a presuppositional deduction based on the belief that the 33 years of Christ's ministry is a repeat of the 33 years of innocence lived by the first Adam.

If this conclusion is not correct, it does not change the Berisheet End-Times Passover Prophecy, it simply disproves one of our presuppositional conclusions that is incidental to the Berisheet End-Times Passover Prophecy.

The 33-year key is important as a prophetic pattern, and it seems to confirm the years Adam spent in innocence based on the years of the 33 years plus of ministry. The 33 key gives us a firm Creation date of 4004 BC. Could this be incorrect? Yes. To be very clear, Creation based on the Berisheet End-Times Passover Prophecy could not have taken place after 4004 BC but it could have taken place as late as 4114 BC without changing the Berisheet End-Times Passover Prophecy.

The only date in question that would change the timeline moving forward is the crucifixion date. We are convinced after years of research that the crucifixion date is 30 AD. But what if we are wrong? What if the date of crucifixion is 33 AD as many believe?

The answer is that you would simply shift all the future dates that are being forecast three years forward.

WHAT'S NEXT?!

If our perspective is correct, then we can expect that the false Messiah will introduce himself to Israel, with a confirmation of a peace treaty right around the year 2023.

If our perspective is correct, then the "Blessed Hope" will be realized sometime between now and the year 2023.

When you boil it all down we are suggesting that the Sabbath Millennial Perspective should not be modified based on the Berisheet Prophetic perspective. This alters the traditional 7000-year Millennial perspective that has always been viewed as starting at Creation. We are suggesting that it should begin from the year 3970 AD, 4000 years looking backward from the Cross of Calvary. The rest is self-evident.

Are the time-stamps discovered in the Berisheet End-Times Passover Prophecy to be taken literally?

We are about to find out!

I can make one claim with absolute certainty.

God's Word will never fail and everything will be done in His perfect time!

If this perspective is proven incorrect by the passage of time, then the error is all mine.

CHAPTER 12

Where will you spend Eternity?

There is NO natural explanation for the Berisheet End-Times Passover Prophecy found in the first six-letter Hebrew word in the Bible. A prophecy that has been hidden for thousands of years in the very first word at the point of the first contact with the mind and heart of fallen man. A prophecy that defies logic and man's reason. It is a supernatural revelation that has been time-locked and just released at the very tail end of this age.

Men today mock the idea that the ancient prophetic text we call the Old and New Testament is literally God's Word.

The very idea that God has placed a special message for those living in the final generation before He is coming again to set up His millennial kingdom is dismissed with a snarky grin and undisguised scorn.

And yet, here it is, proof beyond a reasonable doubt that God poured His plan for the ages, including the inflection point of all history into the first six letters that miraculously contain five additional nested Hebrew words, and a time-stamp that perfectly fits the 7000-year Millennial eschatology. Remember that this millennial perspective is not of modern origin but it the oldest end-times perspective in the world believed by both ancient Rabbis and first century Christian church fathers.

The architecture of this revelation is a work of art. It is as seamless and simple as it is profound. A revelation whose very simplicity is a testimony to its authenticity. A revelation that is forecasting with unquestionable accuracy and time-stamp marker an event whose particulars are known by the entire world. A prophecy that is unassailable as regards to its historicity and breathtaking in its scope of revelation.

There is one mystery in this disclosure that is hard to explain.

Why did God leave this astounding picture and number proof text hidden and out of sight, while in plain sight, for thousands of years?

God could have unveiled it at any time, but yet He kept it sealed up until the very end.

The most amazing prophecy in the Bible and yet hidden from our sight for thousands of years.

Where is the economy in that?

The Lord who produced the best for last at the marriage celebration recorded in the Gospels has done it again.

The best is saved for last.

I believe that there are two reasons for this just as there are two classes of men and women who will be privileged to have this prophetic revelation disclosed to them.

There are two groups of people that will greatly benefit from reading this book. This book was not written for the religious skeptics nor was it written for the mockers and scoffers.

I seriously doubt that anyone in that group would have waded this far into the weeds, as they would have bailed out chapters ago.

If you're reading this then you probably belong to one of the two groups listed below.

One group is made up of those that have already trusted the Lord and are discouraged and downcast as a result of the tidal wave of sin and corruption that has overwhelmed this final generation.

Those that have God's indwelling Spirit know that they are living in a cesspool of depravity.

America was once the place that sent Christian missionaries all over the world to preach the Gospel of Jesus Christ.

That has all changed in the past 100 years, accelerated in the past 50 years and is moving at break-neck speed in the last 10 years.

America today is now the place that produces the gilded pamphlets and roadmaps that entice men and women to abandon God as they enter the pathway that leads to certain destruction and eternal doom.

The good news that Jesus saves lost sinners has been largely replaced with a clarion call to hedonism, paganism, sexual perversion, humanism and every sort of abomination known to man.

America has become Sodom on steroids.

Not content to despoil our own culture, the merchants and missionaries of death and destruction have made it their mission to use all the resources at their disposal to merchandise the very things that caused Lot to be vexed by the sin of Sodom. The very sins now multiplied and exaggerated that brought God's final judgment on Sodom and Gomorrah are crying out for an encore response from Heaven.

Just one atrocity alone would merit unmerciful judgment.

Consider the murder of millions upon untold millions of babies in the womb.

There are places in Chicago, Los Angeles, New Orleans, and Washington DC to name a few, where you're taking your life in your hands if you are outdoors after midnight. But the danger of these places pales in significance to the most dangerous place in the world.

What place is it you might ask?

The answer is the mother's womb which is now the most dangerous place in the world.

Not content to murder our own citizen's children, our government as a matter of policy has incentivized the murder of children in countries all over the earth, making financial aid contingent on the promotion of abortion on demand.

The difference between Sodom and America is that the advancements in communication, science and technology make it possible to extend the reach of depravity in ways that were impossible in previous generations.

The Berisheet End-Times Passover Prophecy reveals a message of hope and comfort to those who are vexed and grieved by what they see cascading and imploding around them.

Nothing catches the Lord by surprise as is evidenced by the hidden prophecy we have just discovered in the first word in the Bible. The Lord knew that those who truly loved him would be in desperate need of encouragement at the very end when the cup of iniquity was just about to overflow and all seemed lost in a sea of iniquity.

Could it be that one of the many ways He is going to encourage those that love and trust Him is with a supernatural prophetic word that was written thousands of years ago for just such a time as this?

A prophetic word that just showed up at the moment most needed in order to encourage and embolden Christians to hang on for just a little while longer.

A prophetic word that emerged not from a dream, a vision, a star map or a contorted collection of biblical data connected in ways so complicated that the ordinary person could not know with any certainty whether it was right or wrong.

NO!

God has given us a prophecy that has now emerged, cocooned from the beginning in His very first revelation to mankind. A prophetic scene displayed with a simplicity that screams authenticity.

Nothing complicated about it.

A clear picture and number message that supports itself with so many fine points of convergence that it would be mathematically impossible to duplicate by random chance.

You might want to go back and read chapters 1-3 with the following question in your mind.

How could this revelation just show up without a Divine hand at work to arrange it so carefully and clearly?

How indeed!

Perhaps He saved it in order to reveal it to a select group of people, using a small Christian publishing house in the US--a publishing house without the reach and influence other mainstream publishers have.

Could you be one of the small remaining remnants that puts their faith and trust in Christ alone? Perhaps you are like the thief on the cross, rescued in the last seconds of time, pulled from the fire just before you are consumed.

There is no more chance that it is an accident that you are reading this book, than the chance that the prophetic harbinger embedded in the first word of the Bible is an accident that has been reserved for the last moments in this age.

Consider that it was placed in plain sight, unseen for thousands of years so that you might be given one final opportunity to change the course of your life. To enter through the door that leads to eternal life through the central person displayed on a wooden cross in the very first word in the Bible, Jesus the Christ.

Listen Up Saints!

What better news, if you are a true-hearted follower of Christ, then the news that His promise to come and take us home is just about to be fulfilled.

What better news for the homesick than the news that we are going HOME!

Listen Up Sinners!

What better news, if you are a sinner who is on the road to hell, then the news that the God of the Universe has made a way for you to escape. What more convincing proof that He loves you than the promise of eternal life. Do you see the outstretched nail-pierced hand of the Savior who is reaching out in order to rescue you from the calamity that is now in the wind and ready to manifest?

A miracle was performed on a wooden cross in order that you might be saved and all you are asked to do is receive it by faith and spend the rest of your life rejoicing in the grace you have received as you glorify God for His Amazing Grace!

The spiritual life of a Christian is not based on believing a creed or saying the right prayer. It is based on a personal relationship with Jesus.

What can you do to enter into this relationship?

There is only one "work" you do. Don't take my word for it. Listen to what Jesus Himself said.

> **JOHN 6:27-29**
> *Labour not for the meat which perisheth, but for that meat which endureth unto everlasting life, which the Son of man shall give unto you: for him hath God the Father sealed. Then said they unto him, What shall we do, that we might work the works of God? Jesus answered and said unto them, This is the work of God, that ye believe on him whom he hath sent.*

If you are a Christian, then the Berisheet End-Times Passover Prophecy is testimony to the fact that everything you believed that was written between the book of Genesis and Revelation is true and trustworthy.

This world is not our home, we are pilgrims on the way to the Celestial City. Like Abraham we are unsettled and always being uprooted in this world as we look with eyes of faith for a city whole maker and builder is God.

The events outlined in the Scriptures that are clearly harbingers of the soon coming of Christ are on the near horizon. The time is short.

If you have checked the box that self-identifies you as a Christian and are comfortable in this world, then you need to begin checking yourself for signs of spiritual life. When the Lord comes to snatch away His invisible church the visible church that goes under the banner of Christendom will largely remain intact and untouched by the "great departure."

The Lord asked a question out loud for our benefit.

Jesus asked, "will I find faith when I come?"

The obvious implication is that saving faith would be a rare commodity when He came to collect His church. Saving faith, by the way, is the only faith that saves.

The vast majority of the visible Christian Church does not believe in, or are they anticipating the rapture of the Church. In fact, they mock and scoff at the very idea of something so absurd.

The only question that really matters a hundred years from now is not whether this millennial prophetic perspective panned out, but rather have you bent the knee, repented of your sins and called on the name of the Lord Jesus Christ to be saved?

One way or another each of us has a date with destiny as it is appointed unto man once to die and after that the judgment.

If death is preempted by the supernatural glorification of our earthly bodies as a result of the departure of the church then the question is will you be going up or left behind?

Are you going to be with Christ forever or separated from Him forever?

The Berishect End-Times Passover Prophecy is simply a preamble to the biblical narrative that has been divinely ordained in order that spiritually homeless men and women might realize the truth that they already know is true: There is a God in Heaven who loves the world, and desires all to be saved. This God is a just judge, and requires perfect holiness, which mankind is incapable of attaining on his own. This same God provided the perfect sacrifice--that of the holy, blameless, Son of the Most High--so that through true, saving faith in Him, we might be reconciled and have everlasting life.

He is coming back very soon!

And just as certainly, the days of your life are numbered.

Which will happen first?

That is a good question, but I have a better one!

Is your name written in the Lamb's Book of Life?

Does the hope of His soon return fill you with joy or dread?

We are all living somewhere on a prescribed and appointed timeline. The Bible teaches that it is appointed unto man once to die and after that the judgment.

Each of us is a heartbeat, a fainting breath, an unexpected moment away from our own final moment in temporal time. My own heart's desire is that if you do not know my amazing Savior that you make HIS acquaintance immediately. Do not wait. Confess your sins, believe in the finished work of Jesus the Christ accomplished on the wooden cross of Calvary and receive the free gift of God's salvation provided by the precious blood of Immanuel who came in human flesh, laying down His own glory so that you might be one day be glorified in order that you might be in His presence forever.

Stop depending upon your own goodness, which God views as filthy rags, and allow the Son of God to clothe you with His Righteousness. Humbly as a child, come into His presence with the simple prayer that He enters your heart and save you from the wrath of God, the wrath you deserve as a rebel and habitual sinner who has up until now rejected the kind and gracious entreaties of the Prince of Heaven.

Sinner COME HOME!

CHECK OUT OUR WEBSITE FOR OTHER TITLES!

www.lighthouse.pub

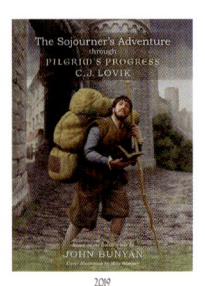

From the editor of the critically acclaimed and recently republished Pilgrim's Progress, author and editor C.J. Lovik brings a unique contribution to the retelling of this classic tale. Lovik brings a fresh and unique view, allowing for a modern audience to read and understand, yet preserving the deep and beloved truths of Bunyan's timeless tale.

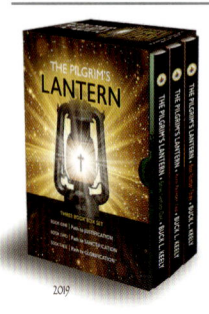

This wonderful three-book box set is a must-have for any new believer, or for anyone desiring to grow deeper in the faith. The series explores three of the major works in the life of a follower of Jesus—Justification, Sanctification, and Glorification.

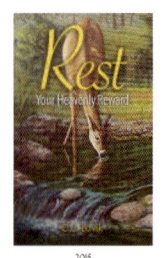

Rest! What is the "rest" that Jesus proclaims in the Book of Matthew as he beckons the weary and burdened to come to him? What is Heaven? How do we get there? What will we do there? What happens when we no longer need the grace of God? These questions, along with many others, are addressed in this brief but powerful book by writer C.J. Lovik.

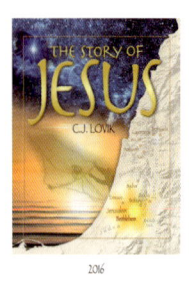

The story of the life of Jesus, as told by four separate biographers, weaves together a harmonized story that accurately portrays the life of Jesus Christ. This book displays the miracle of the four separate accounts, as they each stand without contradiction or discrepancy. Writer C.J. Lovik masterfully overlays these harmonized stories into a single account of the life of the Savior.

www.lighthouse.pub

Visit our website to purchase books, DVDs, and other Christ-centered media, and to preview upcoming titles.

Explore the majesty of the Old Testament Scriptures
with these resources

LIGHTHOUSE GOSPEL BEACON

"Lord reveal yourself to me!" - C.J. Lovik, The Living Word in 3D

www.lighthouse.pub